U.S. Department of Transportation
Federal Aviation Administration

FAA-S-ACS-11A
Includes FAA-G-ACS-2

Airman Certification Standards

Airline Transport Pilot and Type Rating

Airplane

AVIATION SUPPLIES & ACADEMICS, INC.
NEWCASTLE, WASHINGTON

Airline Transport Pilot and Type Rating Airplane Airman Certification Standards

Aviation Supplies & Academics, Inc.
7005 132nd Place SE
Newcastle, Washington 98059
asa@asa2fly.com | 425-235-1500 | asa2fly.com

Visit asa2fly.com/acsupdates for FAA revisions affecting this title.

None of the material in this book supersedes any operational documents or procedures issued by the Federal Aviation Administration.

ASA-ACS-11A
ISBN 978-1-64425-459-2

Additional formats available:
eBook EPUB   ISBN 978-1-64425-460-8
eBook PDF   ISBN 978-1-64425-461-5

Printed in the United States of America

2028 2027 2026 2025 2024   9 8 7 6 5 4 3 2 1

Contents

U.S. Department
of Transportation

**Federal Aviation
Administration**

Airline Transport Pilot and Type Rating
for Airplane Category
Airman Certification Standards

November 2023

Flight Standards Service
Washington, DC 20591

Foreword

The U.S. Department of Transportation, Federal Aviation Administration (FAA), Office of Safety Standards, Regulatory Support Division, Airman Testing Standards Branch has published the Airline Transport Pilot (ATP) for Airplane Category Airman Certification Standards (ACS) to communicate the aeronautical knowledge, risk management, and flight proficiency standards for ATP pilot and type rating certification in the airplane category.

This ACS is available for download, in PDF format, from www.faa.gov.

Comments regarding this ACS may be emailed to acsptsinquiries@faa.gov.

The FAA created FAA-G-ACS-2, Airman Certification Standards Companion Guide for Pilots, to provide guidance considered relevant and useful to the community. The number of appendices in the ACS was reduced and much of the non-regulatory material was moved to the Airman Certification Standards Companion Guide for Pilots. Applicants, instructors, and evaluators should consult this companion guide to familiarize themselves with ACS procedures. FAA-G-ACS-2 is available for download, in PDF format, from www.faa.gov.

Revision History

Document #	Description	Date
FAA-S-8081-5F	Airline Transport Pilot and Type Rating Practical Test Standards for Airplane	July 2008
FAA-S-ACS-11	Airline Transport Pilot and Type Rating for Airplane Airman Certification Standards	May 10, 2019
FAA-S-ACS-11	Airline Transport Pilot and Type Rating for Airplane Airman Certification Standards (Change 1)	May 28, 2019
FAA-S-ACS-11A	Airline Transport Pilot and Type Rating for Airplane Category Airman Certification Standards	November 2023

Major Enhancements to FAA-S-ACS-11A

- The following ACS codes have been added:

AA.I.C.K2a	AA.I.C.K2g	AA.II.D.R7	AA.IV.B.R9
AA.I.C.K2b	AA.I.F.R4	AA.IV.B.R4	AA.VI.F.R10
AA.I.C.K2c	AA.I.G.K7	AA.IV.B.R5	AA.VI.F.R11
AA.I.C.K2d	AA.I.H.K1i	AA.IV.B.R6	AA.VI.H.R8
AA.I.C.K2e	AA.II.C.R6	AA.IV.B.R7	AA.VI.H.R9
AA.I.C.K2f	AA.II.D.R6	AA.IV.B.R8	

- The following ACS codes have been removed and archived. Please see the Airman Certification Standards Companion Guide for Pilots (FAA-G-ACS-2) for more information.

AA.IV.B.R2	AA.V.C.S2	AA.VI.F.R3b	AA.VI.H.R3b
AA.V.A.S2	AA.VI.F.R3	AA.VI.H.R3	AA.VIII.A.R2
AA.V.B.S2	AA.VI.F.R3a	AA.VI.H.R3a	AA.VIII.B.R2

- Non-regulatory material has been moved from the appendices to the Airman Certification Standards Companion Guide for Pilots (FAA-G-ACS-2).
- Legends have been added to the Additional Ratings Task Tables.

Table of Contents

Introduction

Airman Certification Standards Concept

The goal of the airman certification process is to ensure the applicant possesses the knowledge, ability to manage risks, and skill consistent with the privileges of the certificate or rating being exercised, in order to act as pilot-in-command (PIC).

Safe operations in today's National Airspace System (NAS) require the integration of aeronautical knowledge, risk management, and flight proficiency standards. To accomplish these goals, the FAA drew upon the expertise of organizations and individuals across the aviation and training community to develop the ACS. The ACS integrates the elements of knowledge, risk management, and skill required for each airman certificate or rating. It thus forms a more comprehensive standard for what an applicant must know, consider, and do to demonstrate proficiency to pass the tests required for issuance of the applicable airman certificate or rating.

Area of Operation I. Preflight Preparation

Task A. *Operation of Systems*

References: AC 90-117, AC 91.21-1, AC 91-78, AC 120-76; FAA-H-8083-2, FAA-H-8083-3, FAA-H-8083-23, FAA-H-8083-25; FSB Report (type specific); POH/AFM

Objective: To determine the applicant exhibits satisfactory knowledge, risk management, and skills associated with aircraft systems and their components; and their normal, abnormal, and emergency procedures.

Note: See Appendix 3: Aircraft, Equipment, and Operational Requirements & Limitations for information related to this Task.

Knowledge:	The applicant demonstrates understanding of:
AA.I.A.K1	Landing gear–extension/retraction system(s), indicators, float devices, brakes, antiskid, tires, nose-wheel steering, and shock absorbers.
AA.I.A.K2	Powerplant–controls and indications, induction system, carburetor and fuel injection, turbocharging, cooling, mounting points, turbine wheels, compressors, deicing, anti-icing, and other related components.
AA.I.A.K3	Propellers–type, controls, feathering/unfeathering, auto-feather, negative torque sensing, synchronizing, synchrophasing, and thrust reverse, including uncommanded reverse procedures.
AA.I.A.K4	Fuel system–capacity, drains, pumps, controls, indicators, cross-feeding, transferring, jettisoning, fuel grade, color and additives, fueling and defueling procedures, and fuel substitutions.
AA.I.A.K5	Oil system–capacity, allowable types of oil, quantities, and indicators.
AA.I.A.K6	Hydraulic system–capacity, pumps, pressure, reservoirs, allowable types of fluid, and regulators.
AA.I.A.K7	Electrical system–alternators, generators, batteries, circuit breakers and protection devices, controls, indicators, and external and auxiliary power sources and ratings.
AA.I.A.K8	Pneumatic and environmental systems–heating, cooling, ventilation, oxygen, pressurization, supply for ice protection systems, controls, indicators, and regulating devices.
AA.I.A.K9	Avionics and communications–autopilot, flight director, Electronic Flight Instrument Systems (EFIS), Flight Management System (FMS), Electronic Flight Bag (EFB), Radar, Inertial Navigation Systems (INS), Global Navigation Satellite System (GNSS), Space-Based Augmentation System (SBAS), Ground-Based Augmentation System (GBAS), ground-based navigation systems and components, Automatic Dependent Surveillance – Broadcast (ADS-B) In and Out, Automatic Dependent Surveillance – Contract (ADS-C), traffic awareness/warning/ avoidance systems, terrain awareness/warning/alert systems, communication systems (e.g., data link, Ultra High Frequency (UHF)/Very High Frequency (VHF)/High Frequency (HF), satellite), Controller Pilot Data Link Communication (CPDLC), indicating devices, transponder, and emergency locator transmitter, Head Up-Display (HUD).
AA.I.A.K10	Ice protection–anti-ice, deice, pitot-static system protection, turbine inlet, propeller, windshield, airfoil surfaces, and other related components.
AA.I.A.K11	Crewmember and passenger equipment–oxygen system, survival gear, emergency exits, evacuation procedures and crew duties, quick donning oxygen mask for crewmembers, passenger oxygen system.
AA.I.A.K12	Flight controls–ailerons, elevator(s), rudder(s), control tabs, control boost/augmentation systems, flaps, spoilers, leading edge devices, speed brakes, stability augmentation system (e.g., yaw damper), and trim systems.

AA.I.A.K13	Pitot-static system–associated instruments and the power source for those flight instruments. Operation and power sources for other flight instruments.
AA.I.A.K14	Fire & smoke detection, protection, and suppression–powerplant, cargo and passenger compartments, lavatory, pneumatic and environmental, electrical/avionics, and batteries (on aircraft and personal electronic devices).
AA.I.A.K15	Envelope protection–angle of attack warning and protection, and speed protection.
AA.I.A.K16	The contents of the Pilot Owner's Handbook (POH) or Airplane Flight Manual (AFM) with regard to the systems and components in the airplane.
AA.I.A.K17	How to use a Minimum Equipment List (MEL) and a Configuration Deviation List (CDL).

Risk Management: The applicant is able to identify, assess, and mitigate risk associated with:

AA.I.A.R1	Detection of system malfunctions or failures.
AA.I.A.R2	Management of a system failure.
AA.I.A.R3	Monitoring and management of automated systems.
AA.I.A.R4	Following checklists or procedures.

Skills: For the airplane provided for the practical test, the applicant demonstrates the ability to:

AA.I.A.S1	Explain and describe the operation of the aircraft systems and components using correct terminology.
AA.I.A.S2	Recall immediate action items or memory items, if appropriate.
AA.I.A.S3	Identify system or component limitations listed in the POH/AFM.
AA.I.A.S4	Demonstrate or describe, as appropriate, the process for deferring inoperative equipment (e.g., MEL) and using a CDL.
AA.I.A.S5	Comply with operations specifications, management specifications, and letters of authorization, if applicable.
AA.I.A.S6	Through the use of the appropriate checklists and normal and abnormal procedures, demonstrate the proper use of the aircraft systems, subsystems, and devices, as determined by the evaluator.

Task B. Performance and Limitations

References: *14 CFR parts 1, 91; AC 20-117, AC 61-107, AC 61-138, AC 91-74, AC 91-79, AC 120-27, AC 120-58, AC 120-60, AC 135-17; AIM; Chart Supplements; FAA-H-8083-1, FAA-H-8083-2, FAA-H-8083-3, FAA-H-8083-23, FAA-H-8083-25; POH/AFM; SAFO 19001*

Objective: To determine that the applicant exhibits satisfactory knowledge, risk management, and skills associated with operating an aircraft safely within its operating envelope.

Note: *See Appendix 3: Aircraft, Equipment, and Operational Requirements & Limitations for information related to this Task.*

Knowledge: The applicant demonstrates understanding of:

AA.I.B.K1	Elements related to performance and limitations by explaining the use of charts, tables, and data to determine performance.
AA.I.B.K2	How to determine the following, as applicable to the class sought:

AA.I.B.K2a	a. Accelerate-stop / accelerate-go distance
AA.I.B.K2b	b. Takeoff performance [e.g., balance field length and Velocity, Minimum Control (ground) (V_{MCG})]
AA.I.B.K2c	c. Climb performance
AA.I.B.K2d	d. Cruise performance (e.g., optimum and maximum operating altitudes)
AA.I.B.K2e	e. Descent performance
AA.I.B.K2f	f. Landing performance
AA.I.B.K2g	g. Performance with an inoperative powerplant for all phases of flight (AMEL, AMES)
AA.I.B.K2h	h. Weight and balance and how to shift weight
AA.I.B.K3	Factors affecting performance, including:
AA.I.B.K3a	a. Atmospheric conditions
AA.I.B.K3b	b. Pilot technique
AA.I.B.K3c	c. Aircraft configuration (e.g., flap setting)
AA.I.B.K3d	d. Airport environment (e.g., runway condition, land and hold short operations (LAHSO))
AA.I.B.K3e	e. Loading (e.g., center of gravity)
AA.I.B.K3f	f. Aircraft weight
AA.I.B.K4	Aerodynamics and how it relates to performance.
AA.I.B.K5	Adverse effects of exceeding an airplane limitation or the aircraft operating envelope.
AA.I.B.K6	Effects of icing on performance.
AA.I.B.K7	Clean wing concept; deicing and anti-icing procedures, including use of appropriate deice fluid, hold-over tables, calculating hold-over times, and pre-takeoff contamination checks.
AA.I.B.K8	Air carrier weight and balance systems (e.g., average weight program). Air Transport Pilot (ATP) (AMEL, AMES).
AA.I.B.K9	Runway assessment and condition reporting and use of the Runway Condition Assessment Matrix (RCAM). (ATP)(AMEL, AMES).

Risk Management: The applicant is able to identify, assess, and mitigate risk associated with:

AA.I.B.R1	Use of performance charts, tables, and data.
AA.I.B.R2	Airplane limitations.
AA.I.B.R3	Possible differences between calculated performance and actual performance.
AA.I.B.R4	Airplane icing and its effect on performance and stall warning.
AA.I.B.R5	Runway excursions.

Skills: For the airplane provided for the practical test, the applicant demonstrates the ability to:

AA.I.B.S1	Describe the airspeeds used during specific phases of flight.
AA.I.B.S2	Describe the effects of meteorological conditions on performance for all phases of flight and correctly apply these factors to a specific chart, table, graph, or other performance data.
AA.I.B.S3	Describe the procedures for wing contamination recognition and any deice/anti-ice procedures prior to takeoff.

AA.I.B.S4	Explain the adverse effects of airframe icing during all phases of flight. Describe any operating limitations for flight in icing conditions. If equipped, describe the procedures for deicing and anti-icing system use and their effects on performance.
AA.I.B.S5	Compute weight and balance, including practical techniques to resolve out-of-limits calculations for a representative scenario, as specified by the evaluator.
AA.I.B.S6	Determine the computed center-of-gravity is within the acceptable limits and the lateral fuel balance is within limits for takeoff and landing.
AA.I.B.S7	Demonstrate proficient use of appropriate performance charts, tables, graphs, or other data to determine airplane performance and limitations for all phases of flight.

Task C. Weather Information (ATP)

References: *14 CFR part 91; AC 61-107, AC 61-138, AC 91-74, AC 91-92; AIM; FAA-H-8083-2, FAA-H-8083-3, FAA-H-8083-16, FAA-H-8083-25, FAA-H-8083-28*

Objective: To determine the applicant exhibits satisfactory knowledge, risk management, and skills associated with obtaining, understanding, and applying weather information for a flight under IFR.

Note: *If K2 is selected, the evaluator must assess the applicant's knowledge of at least three sub-elements.*

Note: *If K3 is selected, the evaluator must assess the applicant's knowledge of at least three sub-elements.*

Note: *See Appendix 1: Practical Test Roles, Responsibilities, and Outcomes and Appendix 3: Aircraft, Equipment, and Operational Requirements & Limitations for information related to this Task.*

Knowledge:	The applicant demonstrates understanding of:
AA.I.C.K1	Sources of weather data (e.g., National Weather Service, Flight Service) for flight planning purposes.
AA.I.C.K2	Acceptable weather products and resources required for preflight planning, current and forecast weather for departure, en route, and arrival phases of flight such as:
AA.I.C.K2a	a. Airport Observations (METAR and SPECI) and Pilot Observations (PIREP)
AA.I.C.K2b	b. Surface Analysis Chart, Ceiling and Visibility Chart (CVA)
AA.I.C.K2c	c. Terminal Aerodrome Forecasts (TAF)
AA.I.C.K2d	d. Graphical Forecasts for Aviation (GFA)
AA.I.C.K2e	e. Wind and Temperature Aloft Forecast (FB)
AA.I.C.K2f	f. Convective Outlook (AC)
AA.I.C.K2g	g. Inflight Aviation Weather Advisories including Airmen's Meteorological Information (AIRMET), Significant Meteorological Information (SIGMET), and Convective SIGMET
AA.I.C.K3	Meteorology applicable to the departure, en route, alternate, and destination for flights conducted under Instrument Flight Rules (IFR) to include expected climate and hazardous conditions such as:
AA.I.C.K3a	a. Atmospheric composition and stability
AA.I.C.K3b	b. Wind (e.g., windshear, mountain wave, factors affecting wind, etc.)
AA.I.C.K3c	c. Temperature and heat exchange
AA.I.C.K3d	d. Moisture/precipitation
AA.I.C.K3e	e. Weather system formation, including air masses and fronts

AA.I.C.K3f	f. Clouds
AA.I.C.K3g	g. Turbulence
AA.I.C.K3h	h. Thunderstorms and microbursts
AA.I.C.K3i	i. Icing and freezing level information
AA.I.C.K3j	j. Fog/mist
AA.I.C.K3k	k. Frost
AA.I.C.K3l	l. Obstructions to visibility (e.g., smoke, haze, volcanic ash, etc.)
AA.I.C.K4	Flight deck displays of digital weather and aeronautical information, their use to navigate around weather, and equipment limitations.
AA.I.C.K5	Low-visibility operations (e.g., surface movement, category II and III approaches). (ATP) (AMEL, AMES).
AA.I.C.K6	Flight Risk Assessment Tools.

Risk Management:	The applicant is able to identify, assess, and mitigate risk associated with:
AA.I.C.R1	Weather conditions involved in departure and in-flight decision making, to include:
AA.I.C.R1a	a. Circumstances requiring a change in course or destination
AA.I.C.R1b	b. Known or forecast icing, winds or turbulence aloft, volcanic ash, destination weather, etc.
AA.I.C.R1c	c. Personal weather minimums
AA.I.C.R1d	d. Operator specified or aircraft operational limitations, if applicable
AA.I.C.R2	Use and limitations of:
AA.I.C.R2a	a. Installed onboard weather equipment
AA.I.C.R2b	b. Aviation weather reports and forecasts
AA.I.C.R2c	c. Inflight weather resources

Skills:	The applicant exhibits the skill to:
AA.I.C.S1	Interpret weather information, apply principles of aeronautical decision-making, and use a Flight Risk Assessment Tool, if available.

Task D. High-Altitude Aerodynamics (ATP) (AMEL, AMES)

References:	AC 61-107, AC 61-138, AC 120-111; FAA-H-8083-2, FAA-H-8083-3, FAA-H-8083-25
Objective:	To determine the applicant exhibits satisfactory knowledge, risk management, and skills associated with high altitude airplane aerodynamics.
Note:	See Appendix 1: Practical Test Roles, Responsibilities, and Outcomes and Appendix 3: Aircraft, Equipment, and Operational Requirements & Limitations for information related to this Task.

Knowledge:	The applicant demonstrates understanding of:
AA.I.D.K1	Aerodynamics of large transport category airplanes, including flight characteristics of swept wing airplanes (e.g., Mach buffet).
AA.I.D.K2	Energy management.

AA.I.D.K3	Relationship between Mach number, indicated airspeed, true airspeed, and change over altitudes.
AA.I.D.K4	Load factor at high altitude and its effect on high and low speed operating margins.
AA.I.D.K5	Relationship between altitude capability, weight, and temperature.
AA.I.D.K6	Maximum Operating Speed - Knots (V_{MO}) / Maximum Operating Speed - Mach (M_{MO}) convergence and stall angle of attack.
AA.I.D.K7	Maximum Lift over Drag Ratio (L/D_{MAX}).
AA.I.D.K8	Best range and best endurance.
AA.I.D.K9	Factors which contribute to airplane upsets at high altitude and upset prevention and recovery techniques.

Risk Management: The applicant is able to identify, assess, and mitigate risk associated with:

AA.I.D.R1	Managing the airplane's energy state.
AA.I.D.R2	High operating altitudes at high operational weights.
AA.I.D.R3	High altitude slow-downs and excursions behind the power curve.
AA.I.D.R4	Turbulence at high altitude.

Skills: The applicant exhibits the skill to:

AA.I.D.S1	If a cruise altitude is reached, manage the airplane's systems and energy state.

Task E. Air Carrier Operations (ATP) (AMEL, AMES)

References: *14 CFR parts 25, 121; AC 00-46, AC 61-138, AC 91.21-1, AC 91-78, AC 120-51, AC 120-66, AC 120-76, AC 120-82, AC 120-90, AC 120-101; AFM; FAA-H-8083-2, FAA-H-8083-3, FAA-H-8083-25*

Objective: To determine the applicant exhibits satisfactory knowledge, risk management, and skills associated with air carrier operations.

Note: *See Appendix 1: Practical Test Roles, Responsibilities, and Outcomes and Appendix 3: Aircraft, Equipment, and Operational Requirements & Limitations for information related to this Task.*

Knowledge: The applicant demonstrates understanding of:

AA.I.E.K1	Turbine engines, thrust reversing systems, and system malfunctions.
AA.I.E.K2	Airplane automation components (e.g., flight director, autopilot), their relationship to each other, and how to manage the automation for flight.
AA.I.E.K3	Advanced navigation equipment (e.g., FMS, Required Navigation Performance (RNP), ADS-B, EFB, etc.) and how it is used inflight.
AA.I.E.K4	Flightpath warning systems (e.g., Traffic Alert and Collision Avoidance Systems (TCAS), Terrain Awareness and Warning System (TAWS) and how to respond to a warning.
AA.I.E.K5	Altitudes and conditions that require the use of oxygen masks.
AA.I.E.K6	Causes and recognition of cabin pressure loss.
AA.I.E.K7	Appropriate rudder use in transport aircraft to avoid rudder reversal.
AA.I.E.K8	Crew communications (e.g., sterile flight deck rules, briefings).
AA.I.E.K9	Operational control.

AA.I.E.K10	Elements associated with operating at complex and high traffic airports with emphasis on runway incursion prevention techniques.
AA.I.E.K11	Professional responsibilities associated with being an ATP certificate holder and how to apply leadership skills as pilot-in-command.
AA.I.E.K12	Crew resource management (CRM) principles and application in a multi-crew environment.
AA.I.E.K13	Use of safety programs to manage risk across an organization (e.g., Threat and error management (TEM), or Aviation Safety Action Program (ASAP)).
AA.I.E.K14	Operations specifications.

Risk Management: The applicant is able to identify, assess, and mitigate risk associated with:

AA.I.E.R1	Turbine engine and thrust reversing system malfunctions.
AA.I.E.R2	Managing automation and navigation equipment.
AA.I.E.R3	Responding to a flightpath warning system alert.
AA.I.E.R4	Loss of cabin pressure.
AA.I.E.R5	Crew coordination.

Skills: The applicant exhibits the skill to:

AA.I.E.S1	Apply CRM principles and use in a crew environment, as appropriate.

Task F. Human Factors (ATP)

References: AC 60-22, AC 61-107, AC 61-138, AC 120-51, AC 120-100; AIM; FAA-H-8083-2, FAA-H-8083-3, FAA-H-8083-25

Objective: To determine the applicant exhibits satisfactory knowledge, risk management, and skills associated with personal health, flight physiology, and aeromedical and human factors related to safety of flight.

Note: If K1 is selected, the evaluator must assess the applicant's knowledge of at least three sub-elements.

Note: See Appendix 1: Practical Test Roles, Responsibilities, and Outcomes and Appendix 3: Aircraft, Equipment, and Operational Requirements & Limitations for information related to this Task.

Knowledge: The applicant demonstrates understanding of:

AA.I.F.K1	Causes, effects, recognition, and corrective actions associated with aeromedical and physiological issues, including:
AA.I.F.K1a	a. Hypoxia
AA.I.F.K1b	b. Hyperventilation
AA.I.F.K1c	c. Middle ear and sinus problems
AA.I.F.K1d	d. Spatial disorientation
AA.I.F.K1e	e. Motion sickness
AA.I.F.K1f	f. Carbon monoxide poisoning
AA.I.F.K1g	g. Stress
AA.I.F.K1h	h. Fatigue

AA.I.F.K1i	i. Dehydration and nutrition
AA.I.F.K1j	j. Hypothermia
AA.I.F.K1k	k. Optical illusions
AA.I.F.K1l	l. Dissolved nitrogen in the bloodstream after scuba dives
AA.I.F.K2	Effects of alcohol, drugs, and over-the-counter medications.
AA.I.F.K3	Aeronautical Decision-Making (ADM) to include using Crew Resource Management (CRM) or Single-Pilot Resource Management (SRM), as appropriate.
AA.I.F.K4	Components of self-assessment for determining fitness for flight.

Risk Management: The applicant is able to identify, assess, and mitigate risk associated with:

AA.I.F.R1	Aeromedical and physiological issues.
AA.I.F.R2	Hazardous attitudes.
AA.I.F.R3	Distractions, task prioritization, loss of situational awareness, or disorientation.
AA.I.F.R4	Confirmation and expectation bias.

Skills: The applicant exhibits the skill to:

AA.I.F.S1	Perform a self-assessment and determine fitness for flight.

Task G. The Code of Federal Regulations (CFR) (ATP)

References: *14 CFR parts 61, 91, 111, 117, 121, 135; 49 CFR part 830; FAA-H-8083-2, FAA-H-8083-3, FAA-H-8083-25*

Objective: To determine the applicant exhibits satisfactory knowledge associated with regulations applicable to the privileges and limitations of the ATP certificate and to flight operations that require an ATP certificate.

Note: *See Appendix 3: Aircraft, Equipment, and Operational Requirements & Limitations for information related to this Task.*

Note: *See Appendix 1: Practical Test Roles, Responsibilities, and Outcomes and Appendix 3: Aircraft, Equipment, and Operational Requirements & Limitations for information related to this Task.*

Knowledge: The applicant demonstrates understanding of:

AA.I.G.K1	14 CFR part 61, subparts A, B, and G.
AA.I.G.K2	14 CFR part 91 subparts A, B, C, F, G, H.
AA.I.G.K3	14 CFR part 117 (AMEL, AMES).
AA.I.G.K4	14 CFR part 121 subparts A, G, K, M, O, T, U, V (AMEL, AMES).
AA.I.G.K5	14 CFR part 135 subparts A, B, C, D, E, F, G (ASEL, ASES).
AA.I.G.K6	49 CFR part 830.
AA.I.G.K7	14 CFR part 111 subparts A, D.

Risk
Management: The applicant is able to identify, assess, and mitigate risk associated with:

AA.I.G.R1   Lack of compliance with the applicable CFRs.

Skills: The applicant exhibits the skill to:

AA.I.G.S1   Apply the CFRs to the flight and operation.

Task H. Water and Seaplane Characteristics, Seaplane Bases, Maritime Rules, and Aids to Marine Navigation (ASES, AMES)

References: AIM; Chart Supplements; FAA-H-8083-2, FAA-H-8083-3, FAA-H-8083-23, FAA-H-8083-25; POH/AFM; USCG Navigation Rules

Objective: To determine the applicant exhibits satisfactory knowledge, risk management, and skills associated with water and seaplane characteristics, seaplane bases, maritime rules, and aids to marine navigation.

Knowledge: The applicant demonstrates understanding of:

AA.I.H.K1   The characteristics of a water surface as affected by features, such as:

AA.I.H.K1a   a. Size and location

AA.I.H.K1b   b. Protected and unprotected areas

AA.I.H.K1c   c. Surface wind

AA.I.H.K1d   d. Direction and strength of water current

AA.I.H.K1e   e. Floating and partially submerged debris

AA.I.H.K1f   f. Sandbars, islands, and shoals

AA.I.H.K1g   g. Vessel traffic and wakes

AA.I.H.K1h   h. Other characteristics specific to the area

AA.I.H.K1i   i. Direction and height of waves

AA.I.H.K2   Float and hull construction, and its effect on seaplane performance.

AA.I.H.K3   Causes of porpoising and skipping, and the pilot action needed to prevent or correct these occurrences.

AA.I.H.K4   How to locate and identify seaplane bases on charts or in directories.

AA.I.H.K5   Operating restrictions at various bases.

AA.I.H.K6   Right-of-way, steering, and sailing rules pertinent to seaplane operation.

AA.I.H.K7   Marine navigation aids, such as buoys, beacons, lights, sound signals, and range markers.

AA.I.H.K8   Naval vessel protection zones.

AA.I.H.K9   No wake zones.

Risk
Management: The applicant is able to identify, assess, and mitigate risk associated with:

AA.I.H.R1   Local conditions.

AA.I.H.R2   Impact of marine traffic.

| AA.I.H.R3 | Right-of-way and sailing rules pertinent to seaplane operations. |
| AA.I.H.R4 | Limited services and assistance available at seaplane bases. |

Skills: The applicant exhibits the skill to:

AA.I.H.S1	Explain how float and hull construction can affect seaplane performance.
AA.I.H.S2	Describe how to correct for porpoising and skipping.
AA.I.H.S3	Locate seaplane bases on charts or in directories and identify any restrictions.
AA.I.H.S4	Identify marine navigation aids.
AA.I.H.S5	Describe what naval vessel protection zones and no wake zones are.
AA.I.H.S6	Assess the water surface characteristics for the proposed flight.
AA.I.H.S7	Perform correct right-of-way, steering, and sailing operations.

Airline Transport Pilot and Type Rating – Airplane ACS (FAA-S-ACS-11A)

Area of Operation II. Preflight Procedures

Task A. Preflight Assessment

References: 14 CFR parts 43, 61, 63, 71, 91, 97, 117, 119, 121, 135; AC 120-27, AC 120-60, AC 135-17, AIM, FAA-H-8083-2, FAA-H-8083-3, FAA-H-8083-23, FAA-H-8083-25, FAA-H-8083-28; POH/AFM

Objective: To determine the applicant exhibits satisfactory knowledge, risk management, and skills associated with preparation for safe flight.

Note: See Appendix 3: Aircraft, Equipment, and Operational Requirements & Limitations for information related to this Task.

Knowledge:	The applicant demonstrates understanding of:
AA.II.A.K1	Pilot self-assessment.
AA.II.A.K2	Determining that the aircraft to be used is appropriate, airworthy, and in a condition for safe flight by locating and explaining related documents such as:
AA.II.A.K2a	a. Airworthiness and registration certificates
AA.II.A.K2b	b. Operating limitations, handbooks, and manuals
AA.II.A.K2c	c. Minimum Equipment List (MEL) and Configuration Deviation List (CDL), Kinds of Operations Equipment Lists (KOEL)
AA.II.A.K2d	d. Weight and balance data
AA.II.A.K2e	e. Required inspections or tests and appropriate records and documentation (e.g., dispatch release) as applicable to the proposed flight or operation
AA.II.A.K3	Preventive maintenance that can be performed by the pilot or other designated crewmember.
AA.II.A.K4	Aircraft preflight inspection, including:
AA.II.A.K4a	a. Which items should be inspected
AA.II.A.K4b	b. The reasons for checking each item
AA.II.A.K4c	c. How to detect possible defects
AA.II.A.K4d	d. The associated regulations
AA.II.A.K5	Environmental factors, including weather, terrain, route selection, and obstructions.
AA.II.A.K6	Requirements for current and appropriate navigation data.
AA.II.A.K7	Operations specifications, management specifications, or letters of authorization applying to a particular aircraft and operation, if applicable.

Risk Management:	The applicant is able to identify, assess, and mitigate risk associated with:
AA.II.A.R1	Human performance factors.
AA.II.A.R2	Inoperative equipment discovered prior to flight.
AA.II.A.R3	Environment (e.g., weather, airports, airspace, terrain, obstacles).
AA.II.A.R4	External pressures.
AA.II.A.R5	Aviation security concerns.

Skills:	The applicant exhibits the skill to:
AA.II.A.S1	Inspect the aircraft in accordance with an appropriate checklist demonstrating proper operation of applicable airplane systems. Coordinate checklist with crew, if appropriate.

AA.II.A.S2	Coordinate with ground crew and ensure adequate clearance prior to moving doors, hatches, flight control surfaces, etc.
AA.II.A.S3	Document any discrepancies found; take corrective action and acknowledge limitations imposed by MEL/CDL items, if applicable.
AA.II.A.S4	Determine if the aircraft is airworthy and in condition for safe flight.
AA.II.A.S5	Identify and comply with operations specifications as required.
AA.II.A.S6	Assess factors related to the environment (weather, airports, terrain, airspace).
AA.II.A.S7	Ensure the airplane and surfaces are free of ice, snow, and frost. If icing conditions are present, demonstrate satisfactory knowledge of deicing procedures.

Task B. Powerplant Start

References: AIM; FAA-H-8083-2, FAA-H-8083-3, FAA-H-8083-25; POH/AFM

Objective: To determine the applicant exhibits satisfactory knowledge, risk management, and skills associated with powerplant start procedures.

Note: See Appendix 3: Aircraft, Equipment, and Operational Requirements & Limitations for information related to this Task.

Knowledge:	The applicant demonstrates understanding of:
AA.II.B.K1	Normal and abnormal powerplant start procedures and limitations, including the use of an auxiliary power unit (APU) or external power source, if applicable.
AA.II.B.K2	Starting under various conditions.
AA.II.B.K3	Malfunctions during powerplant start, procedures to address the malfunction, and any associated limitations.
AA.II.B.K4	Coordinating and communicating with ground personnel for powerplant start, if applicable.

Risk Management:	The applicant is able to identify, assess, and mitigate risk associated with:
AA.II.B.R1	Malfunctions during powerplant start.
AA.II.B.R2	Propeller and turbine powerplant safety.
AA.II.B.R3	Managing situations where specific instructions or checklist items are not published.
AA.II.B.R4	Personnel, vehicles, vessels, foreign object debris, and other aircraft in the vicinity during powerplant start.

Skills:	The applicant exhibits the skill to:
AA.II.B.S1	Ensure the ground safety procedures are followed during the before-start, start, and after-start phases.
AA.II.B.S2	Use appropriate ground crew personnel during the start procedures (if applicable).
AA.II.B.S3	Coordinate with crew, if applicable, and complete the appropriate checklist(s) prior to and after powerplant start.
AA.II.B.S4	Respond appropriately to an abnormal start or malfunction.

Airline Transport Pilot and Type Rating – Airplane ACS (FAA-S-ACS-11A)

Task C. Taxiing (ASEL, AMEL)

References: 14 CFR parts 91, 121, 135; AC 91-73, AC 120-57, AC 120-74; AIM; Chart Supplements; FAA-H-8083-2, FAA-H-8083-3, FAA-H-8083-25; NOTAMs; POH/AFM

Objective: To determine the applicant exhibits satisfactory knowledge, risk management, and skills associated with safe taxi operations.

Knowledge:	The applicant demonstrates understanding of:
AA.II.C.K1	Current airport aeronautical references and information resources such as the Chart Supplement, airport diagram, and Notices to Air Missions (NOTAMs).
AA.II.C.K2	Taxi instructions/clearances, including published taxi routes.
AA.II.C.K3	Airport markings, signs, and lights.
AA.II.C.K4	Appropriate aircraft lighting for day and night operations.
AA.II.C.K5	Push-back procedures, if applicable.
AA.II.C.K6	Appropriate flight deck activities prior to taxi, including route planning, identifying the location of Hot Spots, and coordinating with crew if, applicable.
AA.II.C.K7	Communications at towered and nontowered airports.
AA.II.C.K8	Entering or crossing runways.
AA.II.C.K9	Night taxi operations.
AA.II.C.K10	Low visibility taxi operations and techniques used to avoid disorientation.
AA.II.C.K11	Single-Engine taxi procedures for (AMEL).

Risk Management:	The applicant is able to identify, assess, and mitigate risk associated with:
AA.II.C.R1	Distractions, task prioritization, loss of situational awareness, or disorientation.
AA.II.C.R2	Confirmation or expectation bias as related to taxi instructions.
AA.II.C.R3	A taxi route or departure runway change.
AA.II.C.R4	Partial completion of checklist(s).
AA.II.C.R5	Low visibility taxi operations.
AA.II.C.R6	Runway incursion.

Skills:	The applicant exhibits the skill to:
AA.II.C.S1	Receive/record taxi instructions, read back/acknowledge taxi clearances, and review taxi routes on the airport diagram.
AA.II.C.S2	Use an appropriate airport diagram or taxi chart, if published.
AA.II.C.S3	Comply with air traffic control (ATC) clearances and instructions and observe all runway hold lines, Instrument Landing System (ILS) critical areas, beacons, and other airport/taxiway markings and lighting.
AA.II.C.S4	Coordinate with crew, if applicable, and complete the appropriate checklist(s) prior to and during taxi, as appropriate.
AA.II.C.S5	Maintain situational awareness.
AA.II.C.S6	Maintain correct and positive airplane control, proper speed, appropriate use of wheel brakes and reverse thrust, and separation between other aircraft, vehicles, and persons to avoid an incursion/ incident/accident.

AA.II.C.S7	Demonstrate taxi during day and night operations. If either condition is not available, the applicant explains the differences between day and night taxi.
AA.II.C.S8	Demonstrate proper use of aircraft exterior lighting for day and night operations. If either condition is not available, the applicant explains the differences between exterior aircraft lighting used for day and night operations.
AA.II.C.S9	Explain the hazards of low visibility taxi operations.

Task D. Taxiing and Sailing (ASES, AMES)

References: 14 CFR part 91, 121, 135; AC 91-73, AC 120-57, AC 120-74; AIM; Chart Supplements; FAA-H-8083-2, FAA-H-8083-3, FAA-H-8083-23, FAA-H-8083-25; POH/AFM

Objective: To determine the applicant exhibits satisfactory knowledge, risk management, and skills associated with safe taxi and sailing operations.

Knowledge:	The applicant demonstrates understanding of:
AA.II.D.K1	Current airport/seaplane base aeronautical references and information resources, including Chart Supplements, airport diagram, and appropriate references.
AA.II.D.K2	Taxi instructions/clearances, if applicable.
AA.II.D.K3	Airport/seaplane base markings, signs, and lights.
AA.II.D.K4	Appropriate aircraft lighting for day and night operations.
AA.II.D.K5	Sailing elements and techniques and when sailing should be used.
AA.II.D.K6	Considerations for determining the most favorable sailing course.
AA.II.D.K7	Airport/seaplane base procedures, including:
AA.II.D.K7a	a. Appropriate flight deck activities prior to taxi or sailing, including route planning, and coordinating with crew, if applicable
AA.II.D.K7b	b. Communications at towered and nontowered seaplane bases
AA.II.D.K7c	c. Entering or crossing runways (land operation)
AA.II.D.K7d	d. Night taxi and sailing operations
AA.II.D.K7e	e. Low visibility taxi and sailing operations

Risk Management:	The applicant is able to identify, assess, and mitigate risk associated with:
AA.II.D.R1	Distractions, task prioritization, loss of situational awareness, or disorientation.
AA.II.D.R2	Porpoising and skipping.
AA.II.D.R3	Partial completion of checklist(s).
AA.II.D.R4	Low visibility taxi and sailing operations.
AA.II.D.R5	Other aircraft, vessels, and hazards.
AA.II.D.R6	Gear position in an amphibious airplane.
AA.II.D.R7	Confirmation or expectation bias as related to taxi instructions.

Skills:	The applicant exhibits the skill to:
AA.II.D.S1	Receive/record taxi instructions, read back/acknowledge taxi clearances, and review taxi routes on the airport diagram.

AA.II.D.S2	Use an appropriate chart during taxi, if published.
AA.II.D.S3	Comply with ATC clearances, as appropriate, and seaplane base/airport/taxiway markings, signals and signs.
AA.II.D.S4	Depart the dock/mooring buoy or beach/ramp in a safe manner, considering wind, current, traffic, and hazards.
AA.II.D.S5	Coordinate with crew, if applicable, and complete the appropriate checklist(s) prior to and during taxi or sailing, as appropriate.
AA.II.D.S6	Maintain situational awareness.
AA.II.D.S7	Maintain correct and positive airplane control, proper speed, appropriate use of reverse thrust, and separation between other aircraft, vehicles, vessels, and persons to avoid an incursion or right-of-way violation.
AA.II.D.S8	Position the flight controls, flaps, doors, water rudders, and power correctly for the existing conditions to follow the desired course while sailing and to prevent or correct for porpoising and skipping during step taxi.
AA.II.D.S9	Use the appropriate idle, plow, or step taxi technique.
AA.II.D.S10	Exhibit procedures for steering and maneuvering while maintaining proper situational awareness and desired orientation, path, and position.
AA.II.D.S11	Plan and follow the most favorable taxi or sailing course for current conditions.
AA.II.D.S12	Demonstrate taxi or sailing during day and night operations. If either condition is not available, the applicant explains the differences between day and night taxi or sailing.
AA.II.D.S13	Demonstrate proper use of aircraft exterior lighting for day and night operations. If either condition is not available, the applicant explains the differences between exterior aircraft lighting used for day and night operations.
AA.II.D.S14	Explain the hazards of low visibility taxi and sailing operations.

Task E. Before Takeoff Checks

References: *FAA-H-8083-2, FAA-H-8083-3, FAA-H-8083-23, FAA-H-8083-25; POH/AFM*

Objective: To determine the applicant exhibits satisfactory knowledge, risk management, and skills associated with before takeoff checks.

Note: *See Appendix 3: Aircraft, Equipment, and Operational Requirements & Limitations for information related to this Task.*

Knowledge:	The applicant demonstrates understanding of:
AA.II.E.K1	Purpose of pre-takeoff checklist items, including:
AA.II.E.K1a	a. Reasons for checking each item
AA.II.E.K1b	b. Detecting malfunctions
AA.II.E.K1c	c. Ensuring the aircraft is in safe operating condition
AA.II.E.K2	Deicing and anti-icing procedures, holdover times, and pre-takeoff contamination check.
AA.II.E.K3	Adverse weather considerations for performance on takeoff (e.g., snow, ice, gusting crosswinds, low-visibility).
AA.II.E.K4	Items to be included in a before takeoff briefing.

**Risk
Management:** The applicant is able to identify, assess, and mitigate risk associated with:

AA.II.E.R1   Division of attention while conducting before takeoff checks.

AA.II.E.R2   An unexpected change in the runway to be used for departure.

AA.II.E.R3   Using performance data to set airspeeds and flight instruments for actual conditions and the departure runway.

AA.II.E.R4   Setting navigation and communication equipment for departure.

AA.II.E.R5   Configuring autopilot and flight director for departure.

AA.II.E.R6   Adverse weather conditions prior to takeoff (e.g., snow, ice, gusting crosswinds, low-visibility).

AA.II.E.R7   Potential powerplant failure during takeoff or other malfunction considering operational factors such as airplane characteristics, runway/takeoff path length, surface conditions, environmental conditions, and obstructions.

Skills: The applicant exhibits the skill to:

AA.II.E.S1   Determine the airplane's takeoff performance for actual conditions and planned departure runway or waterway.

AA.II.E.S2   Coordinate with crew, if applicable, and complete the appropriate checklist(s) prior to takeoff in a timely manner.

AA.II.E.S3   Determine all systems checked are within an acceptable operating range and are safe for the proposed flight. During the checks, explain at the request of the evaluator, any system operating characteristic or limitation and any corrective action for a malfunction.

AA.II.E.S4   Determine airspeeds/V-speeds and set flight instruments appropriately, configure flight director, autopilot, and navigation and communication equipment for the current flight conditions and takeoff and departure clearances.

AA.II.E.S5   Conduct a briefing that includes procedures for emergency and abnormal situations (e.g., powerplant failure, windshear), which may be encountered during takeoff, and state the planned action if they were to occur.

AA.II.E.S6   Obtain and correctly interpret the takeoff and departure clearance.

Area of Operation III. Takeoffs and Landings

Task A. Normal Takeoff and Climb

References: FAA-H-8083-2, FAA-H-8083-3, FAA-H-8083-23, FAA-H-8083-25; POH/AFM

Objective: To determine the applicant exhibits satisfactory knowledge, risk management and skills associated with a normal takeoff and climb.

Note: If a crosswind condition does not exist, the applicant's knowledge of crosswind elements must be evaluated through oral testing.

Note: See Appendix 3: Aircraft, Equipment, and Operational Requirements & Limitations for information related to this Task.

Knowledge:	The applicant demonstrates understanding of:
AA.III.A.K1	Effects of atmospheric conditions, including wind, on takeoff and climb performance.
AA.III.A.K2	Appropriate V-speeds for takeoff and climb.
AA.III.A.K3	Appropriate aircraft configuration and power setting for takeoff and climb.
AA.III.A.K4	Runway markings and lighting.

Risk Management:	The applicant is able to identify, assess, and mitigate risk associated with:
AA.III.A.R1	Selection of a runway, or runway intersection, based on aircraft limitations, available distance, surface conditions, and wind.
AA.III.A.R2	Wake turbulence.
AA.III.A.R3	Abnormal operations, including planning for:
AA.III.A.R3a	a. Rejected takeoff
AA.III.A.R3b	b. Potential engine failure in takeoff/climb phase of flight
AA.III.A.R4	Configuring or setting the aircraft (e.g., trim, flaps, autobrakes, etc.).
AA.III.A.R5	Collision hazards.
AA.III.A.R6	Low altitude maneuvering, including stall, spin, or controlled flight into terrain (CFIT).
AA.III.A.R7	Distractions, task prioritization, loss of situational awareness, or disorientation.

Skills:	The applicant exhibits the skill to:
AA.III.A.S1	Coordinate with crew, if applicable, and complete the appropriate checklist(s) prior to takeoff in a timely manner.
AA.III.A.S2	Make radio calls as appropriate.
AA.III.A.S3	Verify assigned/correct runway (ASEL, AMEL) or takeoff path (ASES, AMES).
AA.III.A.S4	Verify the airplane is configured for takeoff.
AA.III.A.S5	Position the flight controls for the existing wind, if applicable.
AA.III.A.S6	Clear the area, taxi into takeoff position, and align the airplane on the runway centerline (ASEL, AMEL) or takeoff path (ASES, AMES).
AA.III.A.S7	Retract the water rudders, as appropriate (ASES, AMES).
AA.III.A.S8	Establish and maintain the most efficient planing/lift-off attitude, and correct for porpoising or skipping (ASES, AMES).

AA.III.A.S9	Maintain centerline (ASEL, AMEL) and proper flight control inputs during the takeoff roll.
AA.III.A.S10	Confirm takeoff power and proper engine and flight instrument indications prior to rotation making callouts, as appropriate, for the airplane or per the operator's procedures.
AA.III.A.S11	Avoid excessive water spray on the propeller(s) (ASES, AMES).
AA.III.A.S12	Rotate and lift off at the recommended airspeed.
AA.III.A.S13	Establish a power setting and a pitch attitude to maintain the desired climb airspeed/V-speed, ±5 knots for each climb segment.
AA.III.A.S14	Maintain desired heading ±5°.
AA.III.A.S15	Retract the landing gear and flaps in accordance with manufacturer or operator procedures and limitations, as appropriate.
AA.III.A.S16	Avoid wake turbulence, if applicable.
AA.III.A.S17	Follow noise abatement procedures, as practicable.
AA.III.A.S18	Complete appropriate after takeoff checklist(s) in a timely manner.

Task B. Normal Approach and Landing

References: AIM; FAA-H-8083-2, FAA-H-8083-3, FAA-H-8083-23, FAA-H-8083-25; POH/AFM; SAFO 17010, SAFO 19001

Objective: To determine the applicant exhibits satisfactory knowledge, risk management, and skills associated with a normal approach and landing.

Note: If a crosswind condition does not exist, the applicant's knowledge of crosswind elements must be evaluated through oral testing.

Note: See Appendix 3: Aircraft, Equipment, and Operational Requirements & Limitations for information related to this Task.

Knowledge:	The applicant demonstrates understanding of:
AA.III.B.K1	A stabilized approach, including energy management concepts.
AA.III.B.K2	Effects of atmospheric conditions, including wind, on approach and landing performance.
AA.III.B.K3	Wind correction techniques on approach and landing.
AA.III.B.K4	Runway markings and lighting.

Risk Management:	The applicant is able to identify, assess, and mitigate risk associated with:
AA.III.B.R1	Selection of a runway or approach path and touchdown area based on aircraft limitations, available distance, surface conditions, and wind.
AA.III.B.R2	Wake turbulence.
AA.III.B.R3	Go-around/rejected landing.
AA.III.B.R4	Land and hold short operations (LAHSO).
AA.III.B.R5	Collision hazards.
AA.III.B.R6	Low altitude maneuvering, including stall, spin, or controlled flight into terrain (CFIT).
AA.III.B.R7	Distractions, loss of situational awareness, incorrect airport surface approach and landing, or improper task management.

Skills: The applicant exhibits the skill to:

AA.III.B.S1   Coordinate with crew, if applicable, and complete the appropriate checklist(s).

AA.III.B.S2   Make radio calls as appropriate.

AA.III.B.S3   Maintain a ground track that ensures the desired traffic pattern flown takes into consideration obstructions and air traffic control (ATC) or evaluator instructions.

AA.III.B.S4   Ensure the airplane is aligned with the correct/assigned runway or landing surface.

AA.III.B.S5   Scan the runway or landing surface and adjoining area for traffic and obstructions.

AA.III.B.S6   Select a suitable touchdown point considering wind, landing surface, and obstructions.

AA.III.B.S7   Establish the recommended approach and landing configuration and airspeed, ±5 knots, and adjust pitch attitude and power as required to maintain a stabilized approach.

AA.III.B.S8   Maintain directional control and appropriate crosswind correction throughout the approach and landing.

AA.III.B.S9   Make smooth, timely, and correct control application before, during, and after touchdown.

AA.III.B.S10   Touch down with the runway centerline between the main landing gear at the appropriate speed and pitch attitude at the runway aiming point markings -250/+500 feet, or where there are no runway markings 750 to 1,500 feet from the approach threshold of the runway (ASEL, AMEL).

AA.III.B.S11   During round out and touchdown contact the water at the proper pitch attitude within 200 feet beyond a specified point (ASES, AMES). In addition, for AMES, the touchdown is within the first one-third of the water landing area.

AA.III.B.S12   Decelerate to taxi speed (20 knots or less on dry pavement, 10 knots or less on contaminated pavement) to within the calculated landing distance plus 25% for the actual conditions with the runway centerline between the main landing gear (At least one landing) (ASEL, AMEL).

AA.III.B.S13   Use spoilers, prop reverse, thrust reverse, wheel brakes, and other drag/braking devices, as appropriate to safely slow the airplane. (At least one landing to a full stop).

AA.III.B.S14   Execute a timely go-around if the approach cannot be made within the tolerances specified above or for any other condition that may result in an unsafe approach or landing.

AA.III.B.S15   Use runway incursion avoidance procedures, if applicable.

Task C. Glassy Water Takeoff and Climb (ASES, AMES)

References: *FAA-H-8083-2, FAA-H-8083-3, FAA-H-8083-23, FAA-H-8083-25; POH/AFM*

Objective: To determine the applicant exhibits satisfactory knowledge, risk management, and skills associated with glassy water takeoff and climb.

Note: *If a glassy water condition does not exist, the applicant must be evaluated by simulating the Task.*

Note: *See Appendix 3: Aircraft, Equipment, and Operational Requirements & Limitations for information related to this Task.*

Knowledge: The applicant demonstrates understanding of:

AA.III.C.K1   Effects of atmospheric conditions, including wind, on takeoff and climb performance.

AA.III.C.K2   Appropriate power settings and V-speeds for takeoff and climb.

AA.III.C.K3   Appropriate airplane configuration.

AA.III.C.K4   Appropriate use of glassy water takeoff and climb technique.

Risk Management: The applicant is able to identify, assess, and mitigate risk associated with:

AA.III.C.R1	Selection of the takeoff path based on aircraft limitations, available distance, surface conditions, and wind.
AA.III.C.R2	Abnormal operations, including planning for:
AA.III.C.R2a	a. Rejected takeoff
AA.III.C.R2b	b. Potential engine failure in takeoff/climb phase of flight
AA.III.C.R3	Collision hazards.
AA.III.C.R4	Low altitude maneuvering, including stall, spin, or controlled flight into terrain (CFIT).
AA.III.C.R5	Distractions, task prioritization, loss of situational awareness, or disorientation.
AA.III.C.R6	Gear position in an amphibious airplane.

Skills: The applicant exhibits the skill to:

AA.III.C.S1	Coordinate with crew, if applicable, and complete the appropriate checklist(s) prior to takeoff in a timely manner.
AA.III.C.S2	Make radio calls as appropriate.
AA.III.C.S3	Position the flight controls for the existing wind, if applicable.
AA.III.C.S4	Verify the airplane is configured for takeoff.
AA.III.C.S5	Clear the area; select appropriate takeoff path considering surface conditions and collision hazards.
AA.III.C.S6	Retract the water rudders, as appropriate.
AA.III.C.S7	Set and confirm takeoff power.
AA.III.C.S8	Avoid excessive water spray on the propeller(s).
AA.III.C.S9	Maintain directional control throughout takeoff and climb.
AA.III.C.S10	Establish and maintain an appropriate planing attitude, directional control, and correct for porpoising, skipping, and increase in water drag.
AA.III.C.S11	Utilize appropriate techniques to lift seaplane from the water considering surface conditions.
AA.III.C.S12	Adjust power, as appropriate, and establish a pitch attitude to maintain the appropriate climb airspeed/V-speed, ±5 knots for each climb segment.
AA.III.C.S13	Retract flaps after a positive rate of climb has been verified or in accordance with manufacturer or operator procedures and limitations, as appropriate.
AA.III.C.S14	Follow noise abatement procedures, as practicable.

Task D. Glassy Water Approach and Landing (ASES, AMES)

References: *FAA-H-8083-2, FAA-H-8083-3, FAA-H-8083-23, FAA-H-8083-25; POH/AFM*

Objective: To determine the applicant exhibits satisfactory knowledge, risk management, and skills associated with glassy water approach and landing.

Note: *If a glassy water condition does not exist, the applicant must be evaluated by simulating the Task.*

Note: *See Appendix 3: Aircraft, Equipment, and Operational Requirements & Limitations for information related to this Task.*

Knowledge:	The applicant demonstrates understanding of:
AA.III.D.K1	A stabilized approach, including energy management concepts.
AA.III.D.K2	Effects of atmospheric conditions, including wind, on approach and landing performance.
AA.III.D.K3	Wind correction techniques on approach and landing.
AA.III.D.K4	When and why glassy water techniques are used.
AA.III.D.K5	How a glassy water approach and landing is executed.

Risk Management:	The applicant is able to identify, assess, and mitigate risk associated with:
AA.III.D.R1	Selection of the approach path and touchdown area based on aircraft limitations, available distance, surface conditions, and wind.
AA.III.D.R2	Go-around/rejected landing.
AA.III.D.R3	Collision hazards.
AA.III.D.R4	Low altitude maneuvering, including stall, spin, or controlled flight into terrain (CFIT).
AA.III.D.R5	Distractions, task prioritization, loss of situational awareness, or disorientation.
AA.III.D.R6	Gear position in an amphibious airplane.

Skills:	The applicant exhibits the skill to:
AA.III.D.S1	Coordinate with crew, if applicable, and complete the appropriate checklist(s).
AA.III.D.S2	Make radio calls as appropriate.
AA.III.D.S3	Ensure that the landing gear and water rudders are retracted, if applicable.
AA.III.D.S4	Consider the landing surface, visual attitude references, water depth, and collision hazards and select the proper approach and landing path.
AA.III.D.S5	Establish the recommended approach and landing configuration, airspeed, and trim, and adjust pitch attitude and power as required to maintain a stabilized approach.
AA.III.D.S6	Maintain a stabilized approach and recommended airspeed, ±5 knots.
AA.III.D.S7	Make smooth, timely, and correct power and control adjustments to maintain proper pitch attitude and rate of descent to touchdown.
AA.III.D.S8	Maintain directional control throughout the approach and landing.
AA.III.D.S9	Contact the water in a proper pitch attitude, and slow to idle taxi speed.

Task E. Rough Water Takeoff and Climb (ASES, AMES)

References: *FAA-H-8083-2, FAA-H-8083-3, FAA-H-8083-23, FAA-H-8083-25; POH/AFM*

Objective: To determine the applicant exhibits satisfactory knowledge, risk management, and skills associated with rough water takeoff and climb.

Note: *If a rough water condition does not exist, the applicant must be evaluated by simulating the Task.*

Note: *See Appendix 3: Aircraft, Equipment, and Operational Requirements & Limitations for information related to this Task.*

Knowledge:	The applicant demonstrates understanding of:
AA.III.E.K1	Effects of atmospheric conditions, including wind, on takeoff and climb performance.

AA.III.E.K2	Appropriate power settings and V-speeds for takeoff and climb.
AA.III.E.K3	Appropriate airplane configuration.
AA.III.E.K4	Appropriate use of rough water takeoff and climb technique.

Risk Management: The applicant is able to identify, assess, and mitigate risk associated with:

AA.III.E.R1	Selection of the takeoff path based on aircraft limitations, available distance, surface conditions, and wind.
AA.III.E.R2	Abnormal operations, including planning for:
AA.III.E.R2a	a. Rejected takeoff
AA.III.E.R2b	b. Potential engine failure in takeoff/climb phase of flight
AA.III.E.R3	Collision hazards.
AA.III.E.R4	Low altitude maneuvering, including stall, spin, or controlled flight into terrain (CFIT).
AA.III.E.R5	Distractions, task prioritization, loss of situational awareness, or disorientation.
AA.III.E.R6	Gear position in an amphibious airplane.

Skills: The applicant exhibits the skill to:

AA.III.E.S1	Coordinate with crew, if applicable, and complete the appropriate checklist(s) prior to takeoff in a timely manner.
AA.III.E.S2	Make radio calls as appropriate.
AA.III.E.S3	Position the flight controls for the existing wind, if applicable.
AA.III.E.S4	Verify the airplane is configured for takeoff.
AA.III.E.S5	Clear the area; select appropriate takeoff path considering surface conditions and collision hazards.
AA.III.E.S6	Retract the water rudders, as appropriate.
AA.III.E.S7	Set and confirm takeoff power.
AA.III.E.S8	Avoid excessive water spray on the propeller(s).
AA.III.E.S9	Maintain directional control and proper wind-drift correction throughout takeoff and climb.
AA.III.E.S10	Establish and maintain an appropriate planing attitude, directional control, and correct for porpoising, skipping, and increase in water drag.
AA.III.E.S11	Establish proper attitude and airspeed, lift off at minimum airspeed and accelerate to appropriate climb airspeed/V-speed, ±5 knots before leaving ground effect.
AA.III.E.S12	Retract the flaps after a positive rate of climb is established and a safe altitude has been achieved.
AA.III.E.S13	Maintain takeoff power to a safe maneuvering altitude then set climb power.
AA.III.E.S14	Follow noise abatement procedures, as practicable.

Task F. Rough Water Approach and Landing (ASES, AMES)

References: FAA-H-8083-2, FAA-H-8083-3, FAA-H-8083-23, FAA-H-8083-25; POH/AFM

Objective: To determine the applicant exhibits satisfactory knowledge, risk management, and skills associated with rough water approach and landing.

Note: If a rough water condition does not exist, the applicant must be evaluated by simulating the Task.

Note: See Appendix 3: Aircraft, Equipment, and Operational Requirements & Limitations for information related to this Task.

Knowledge:	The applicant demonstrates understanding of:
AA.III.F.K1	A stabilized approach, including energy management concepts.
AA.III.F.K2	Effects of atmospheric conditions, including wind, on approach and landing performance.
AA.III.F.K3	Wind correction techniques on approach and landing.
AA.III.F.K4	When and why rough water techniques are used.
AA.III.F.K5	How to perform a proper rough water approach and landing.

Risk Management:	The applicant is able to identify, assess, and mitigate risk associated with:
AA.III.F.R1	Selection of the approach path and touchdown area based on airplane limitations, available distance, surface conditions, and wind.
AA.III.F.R2	Go-around/rejected landing.
AA.III.F.R3	Collision hazards.
AA.III.F.R4	Low altitude maneuvering, including stall, spin, or controlled flight into terrain (CFIT).
AA.III.F.R5	Distractions, task prioritization, loss of situational awareness, or disorientation.
AA.III.F.R6	Gear position in an amphibious airplane.

Skills:	The applicant exhibits the skill to:
AA.III.F.S1	Coordinate with crew, if applicable, and complete the appropriate checklist(s).
AA.III.F.S2	Make radio calls as appropriate.
AA.III.F.S3	Ensure that the landing gear and water rudders are retracted, if applicable.
AA.III.F.S4	Consider the landing surface, visual attitude references, water depth, and collision hazards and select the proper approach and landing path.
AA.III.F.S5	Establish the recommended approach and landing configuration, airspeed, and trim, and adjust pitch attitude and power as required to maintain a stabilized approach.
AA.III.F.S6	Maintain a stabilized approach and recommended airspeed with gust factor applied, ±5 knots.
AA.III.F.S7	Make smooth, timely, and correct power and control adjustments to maintain proper attitude and rate of descent to touchdown.
AA.III.F.S8	Contact the water at the correct pitch attitude and touchdown speed.
AA.III.F.S9	Make smooth, timely, and correct power and control application during the landing while remaining alert for a go-around should conditions be too rough.
AA.III.F.S10	Maintain positive after-landing control.

Task G. Confined Area Takeoff and Maximum Performance Climb (ASES, AMES)

References: FAA-H-8083-2, FAA-H-8083-3, FAA-H-8083-23, FAA-H-8083-25; POH/AFM

Objective: To determine the applicant exhibits satisfactory knowledge, risk management, and skills associated with confined area takeoff and maximum performance climb.

Note: See Appendix 3: Aircraft, Equipment, and Operational Requirements & Limitations for information related to this Task.

Knowledge:	The applicant demonstrates understanding of:
AA.III.G.K1	Effects of atmospheric conditions, including wind, on takeoff and climb performance.
AA.III.G.K2	Appropriate power settings and V-speeds for takeoff and climb.
AA.III.G.K3	Appropriate airplane configuration.
AA.III.G.K4	Effects of water surface.
AA.III.G.K5	Available techniques for confined-area takeoff and climb.

Risk Management:	The applicant is able to identify, assess, and mitigate risk associated with:
AA.III.G.R1	Selection of the takeoff path based on airplane limitations, available distance, surface conditions, and wind.
AA.III.G.R2	Abnormal operations, including planning for:
AA.III.G.R2a	a. Rejected takeoff
AA.III.G.R2b	b. Potential engine failure in takeoff/climb phase of flight
AA.III.G.R3	Collision hazards.
AA.III.G.R4	Low altitude maneuvering, including stall, spin, or controlled flight into terrain (CFIT).
AA.III.G.R5	Distractions, task prioritization, loss of situational awareness, or disorientation.
AA.III.G.R6	Gear position in an amphibious airplane.

Skills:	The applicant exhibits the skill to:
AA.III.G.S1	Coordinate with crew, if applicable, and complete the appropriate checklist(s) prior to takeoff in a timely manner.
AA.III.G.S2	Make radio calls as appropriate.
AA.III.G.S3	Position the flight controls for the existing wind, if applicable.
AA.III.G.S4	Verify the airplane is configured for takeoff.
AA.III.G.S5	Clear the area; select appropriate takeoff path considering surface conditions and collision hazards.
AA.III.G.S6	Retract the water rudders, as appropriate.
AA.III.G.S7	Set and confirm takeoff power.
AA.III.G.S8	Avoid excessive water spray on the propeller(s).
AA.III.G.S9	Maintain directional control and proper wind-drift correction throughout takeoff and climb.
AA.III.G.S10	Establish and maintain an appropriate planing attitude, directional control, and correct for porpoising, skipping, and increase in water drag.
AA.III.G.S11	Rotate and lift off at the appropriate airspeed, and accelerate to the recommended obstacle clearance airspeed or V_X using appropriate bank angles to maintain terrain clearance, as needed.

AA.III.G.S12 Climb at the recommended airspeed or in its absence at best angle-of-climb speed (V_X), +5/-0 knots until the obstacle is cleared, or until the airplane is 50 feet above the surface. In multiengine airplanes with V_X values within 5 knots of minimum control speed (V_{MC}), the use of best rate of climb speed (V_Y) or the manufacturer's recommendation is acceptable.

AA.III.G.S13 After clearing all obstacles, accelerate to V_Y ±5 knots.

AA.III.G.S14 Retract flaps and adjust power as needed to maintain V_Y or appropriate climb airspeed, ±5 knots to a safe maneuvering altitude.

AA.III.G.S15 Follow noise abatement procedures, as practicable.

Task H. Confined Area Approach and Landing (ASES, AMES)

References: FAA-H-8083-2, FAA-H-8083-3, FAA-H-8083-23, FAA-H-8083-25; POH/AFM

Objective: To determine the applicant exhibits satisfactory knowledge, risk management, and skills associated with confined area approach and landing.

Note: See Appendix 3: Aircraft, Equipment, and Operational Requirements & Limitations for information related to this Task.

Knowledge:	The applicant demonstrates understanding of:
AA.III.H.K1	A stabilized approach, including energy management concepts.
AA.III.H.K2	Effects of atmospheric conditions, including wind, on approach and landing performance.
AA.III.H.K3	Available techniques for confined-area approach and landing.
AA.III.H.K4	Wind correction techniques on approach and landing.

Risk Management:	The applicant is able to identify, assess, and mitigate risk associated with:
AA.III.H.R1	Selection of the approach path and touchdown area based on aircraft limitations, available distance, surface conditions, and wind.
AA.III.H.R2	Go-around/rejected landing.
AA.III.H.R3	Collision hazards.
AA.III.H.R4	Low altitude maneuvering, including stall, spin, or controlled flight into terrain (CFIT).
AA.III.H.R5	Distractions, task prioritization, loss of situational awareness, or disorientation.
AA.III.H.R6	Gear position in an amphibious airplane.
AA.III.H.R7	Landing in an area or in conditions where a takeoff/climb may not be possible.

Skills:	The applicant exhibits the skill to:
AA.III.H.S1	Coordinate with crew, if applicable, and complete the appropriate checklist(s).
AA.III.H.S2	Make radio calls as appropriate.
AA.III.H.S3	Ensure that the landing gear and water rudders are retracted, if applicable.
AA.III.H.S4	Consider the landing surface, visual attitude references, water depth, and collision hazards and select the proper approach and landing path.
AA.III.H.S5	Establish the recommended approach and landing configuration, airspeed, and trim, and adjust pitch attitude and power as required to maintain a stabilized approach.
AA.III.H.S6	Maintain a stabilized approach and recommended airspeed with gust factor applied, ±5 knots.

AA.III.H.S7	Make smooth, timely, and correct power and control adjustments to maintain proper attitude and rate of descent to touchdown.
AA.III.H.S8	Touch down smoothly at the recommended airspeed and pitch attitude, beyond and within 100 feet of a specified point/area.
AA.III.H.S9	Maintain directional control and appropriate crosswind correction throughout the approach and landing.

Task I. Rejected Takeoff

References: *FAA-H-8083-2, FAA-H-8083-3, FAA-H-8083-23, FAA-H-8083-25; POH/AFM*

Objective: To determine the applicant exhibits satisfactory knowledge, risk management, and skills associated with a rejected takeoff.

Note: *See Appendix 2: Safety of Flight and Appendix 3: Aircraft, Equipment, and Operational Requirements & Limitations for information related to this Task.*

Knowledge:	The applicant demonstrates understanding of:
AA.III.I.K1	Conditions and situations that could warrant a rejected takeoff (e.g., takeoff warning systems, powerplant failure, other systems warning/failure).
AA.III.I.K2	Safety considerations following a rejected takeoff.
AA.III.I.K3	The procedure for accomplishing a rejected takeoff.
AA.III.I.K4	Accelerate/stop distance.
AA.III.I.K5	Relevant V-speeds for a rejected takeoff.

Risk Management:	The applicant is able to identify, assess, and mitigate risk associated with:
AA.III.I.R1	Selection of the takeoff path based on aircraft limitations, available distance, surface conditions, and wind.
AA.III.I.R2	A powerplant failure or other malfunction during takeoff.
AA.III.I.R3	Directional control following a rejected takeoff.
AA.III.I.R4	A rejected takeoff with inadequate stopping distance.
AA.III.I.R5	High-speed rejected takeoff.
AA.III.I.R6	Distractions, task prioritization, loss of situational awareness, or disorientation.

Skills:	The applicant exhibits the skill to:
AA.III.I.S1	Reject the takeoff if the powerplant failure occurs prior to becoming airborne (ASEL, ASES).
AA.III.I.S2	Reject the takeoff if the powerplant failure occurs at a point during the takeoff where the rejected takeoff procedure can be initiated and the airplane can be safely stopped on the remaining runway/waterway (AMEL, AMES).
AA.III.I.S3	Promptly reduce the power and maintain positive aircraft control using drag and braking devices, as appropriate, to come to a stop.
AA.III.I.S4	Coordinate with crew, if applicable, and complete the appropriate procedures, checklist(s), and radio calls following a rejected takeoff in a timely manner.

Task J. Go-Around/Rejected Landing

References: AIM; FAA-H-8083-2, FAA-H-8083-3, FAA-H-8083-23, FAA-H-8083-25; FSB Report (type specific); POH/AFM

Objective: To determine the applicant exhibits satisfactory knowledge, risk management, and skills associated with a go-around/rejected landing.

Note: See Appendix 3: Aircraft, Equipment, and Operational Requirements & Limitations for information related to this Task.

Knowledge:	The applicant demonstrates understanding of:
AA.III.J.K1	A stabilized approach, including energy management concepts.
AA.III.J.K2	Effects of atmospheric conditions, including wind and density altitude, on a go-around or rejected landing.
AA.III.J.K3	Wind correction techniques on takeoff/departure and approach/landing.
AA.III.J.K4	Situations and considerations on approach that could require a go-around/rejected landing, including the inability to comply with a LAHSO clearance.
AA.III.J.K5	Go-around/rejected landing procedures, the importance of a timely decision, and appropriate airspeed/V-speeds for the maneuver.

Risk Management:	The applicant is able to identify, assess, and mitigate risk associated with:
AA.III.J.R1	Delayed recognition of the need for a go-around/rejected landing.
AA.III.J.R2	Delayed performance of a go-around at low altitude.
AA.III.J.R3	Power application.
AA.III.J.R4	Configuring the airplane.
AA.III.J.R5	Collision hazards.
AA.III.J.R6	Low altitude maneuvering, including stall, spin, or controlled flight into terrain (CFIT).
AA.III.J.R7	Distractions, task prioritization, loss of situational awareness, or disorientation.
AA.III.J.R8	Managing a go-around/rejected landing after accepting a LAHSO clearance.

Skills:	The applicant exhibits the skill to:
AA.III.J.S1	Make a timely decision to go-around/reject the landing.
AA.III.J.S2	Apply the appropriate power setting for the flight condition and establish a pitch attitude necessary to obtain the desired performance.
AA.III.J.S3	Establish a positive rate of climb and the appropriate airspeed/V-speed, ±5 knots.
AA.III.J.S4	Configure and trim the airplane, when appropriate.
AA.III.J.S5	Make radio calls as appropriate.
AA.III.J.S6	Maintain the ground track, heading, or course appropriate for the conditions, or as specified by ATC or the evaluator.
AA.III.J.S7	Complete the appropriate procedures and checklist(s) in a timely manner.

Area of Operation IV. In-flight Maneuvers

Task A. Steep Turns

References: FAA-H-8083-2, FAA-H-8083-3, FAA-H-8083-25; FSB Report (type specific); POH/AFM

Objective: To determine the applicant exhibits satisfactory knowledge, risk management, and skills associated with steep turns.

Note: See Appendix 3: Aircraft, Equipment, and Operational Requirements & Limitations for information related to this Task.

Knowledge:	The applicant demonstrates understanding of:
AA.IV.A.K1	Energy management concepts.
AA.IV.A.K2	Aerodynamics associated with steep turns, including:
AA.IV.A.K2a	a. Maintaining coordinated flight
AA.IV.A.K2b	b. Overbanking tendencies
AA.IV.A.K2c	c. Maneuvering speed, including the impact of weight changes
AA.IV.A.K2d	d. Load factor and accelerated stalls
AA.IV.A.K2e	e. Rate and radius of turn

Risk Management:	The applicant is able to identify, assess, and mitigate risk associated with:
AA.IV.A.R1	Spatial disorientation when conducting a steep turn while flying by reference to instruments.
AA.IV.A.R2	Collision hazards including aircraft and terrain.
AA.IV.A.R3	Low altitude maneuvering, including stall, spin, or controlled flight into terrain (CFIT).
AA.IV.A.R4	Distractions, task prioritization, loss of situational awareness, or disorientation.
AA.IV.A.R5	Uncoordinated flight.

Skills:	The applicant exhibits the skill to:
AA.IV.A.S1	Select an entry altitude that allows the Task to be completed no lower than 3,000 feet above ground level (AGL).
AA.IV.A.S2	Establish the manufacturer's recommended airspeed; or if one is not available, an airspeed not to exceed maneuvering speed (V_A).
AA.IV.A.S3	Establish at least a 45° bank solely by reference to instruments and make a coordinated steep turn of at least 180°, as specified by the evaluator.
AA.IV.A.S4	Perform the Task in the opposite direction, as specified by evaluator.
AA.IV.A.S5	Make smooth pitch, bank, and power adjustments as needed.
AA.IV.A.S6	Maintain the entry altitude ±100 feet, airspeed ±10 knots, bank ±5°, and roll out on the specified heading, ±10°.
AA.IV.A.S7	Avoid any indication of an impending stall, abnormal flight attitude, or exceeding any structural or operating limitation during any part of the Task.

Task B. Recovery from Unusual Flight Attitudes

References: *AC 120-111; FAA-H-8083-2, FAA-H-8083-15, FAA-H-8083-25; FSB Report (type specific); POH/AFM*

Objective: To determine the applicant exhibits satisfactory knowledge, risk management, and skills associated with recovering from unusual flight attitudes solely by reference to instruments.

Knowledge:	The applicant demonstrates understanding of:
AA.IV.B.K1	Procedures for recovery from unusual flight attitudes.
AA.IV.B.K2	Unusual flight attitude causal factors, including physiological factors, system and equipment failures, and environmental factors.
AA.IV.B.K3	The operating envelope and structural limitations for the aircraft.
AA.IV.B.K4	Effects of engine location, wing design, and other specific design characteristics that could affect aircraft control during the recovery.

Risk Management:	The applicant is able to identify, assess, and mitigate risk associated with:
AA.IV.B.R1	Situations that could lead to loss of control in-flight (LOC-I) or unusual attitudes in-flight (e.g., stress, task saturation, inadequate instrument scan distractions, and spatial disorientation).
AA.IV.B.R2	[Archived]
AA.IV.B.R3	Operating envelope considerations.
AA.IV.B.R4	Interpreting flight instruments.
AA.IV.B.R5	Assessment of the unusual attitude.
AA.IV.B.R6	Control input errors, inducing undesired aircraft attitudes.
AA.IV.B.R7	Control application solely by reference to instruments.
AA.IV.B.R8	Collision hazards.
AA.IV.B.R9	Distractions, task prioritization, loss of situational awareness, or disorientation.

Skills:	The applicant exhibits the skill to:
AA.IV.B.S1	Use proper instrument cross-check and interpretation to identify an unusual attitude (including both nose-high and nose-low) in flight, and apply the appropriate flight control, power input, and aircraft configuration in the correct sequence, to return to a stabilized level flight attitude.

Task C. Specific Flight Characteristics

References: *FAA-H-8083-2, FAA-H-8083-3, FAA-H-8083-25; FSB Report (type specific); POH/AFM*

Objective: To determine the applicant exhibits satisfactory knowledge, risk management, and skills associated with flight and performance characteristics unique to a specific aircraft type.

Note: *See Appendix 3: Aircraft, Equipment, and Operational Requirements & Limitations for information related to this Task.*

Knowledge:	The applicant demonstrates understanding of:
AA.IV.C.K1	All specific flight and performance characteristics associated with the aircraft.

Risk Management:	The applicant is able to identify, assess, and mitigate risk associated with:

AA.IV.C.R1   Specific flight and performance characteristics, their effects, and applicable procedures.

AA.IV.C.R2   Distractions, task prioritization, loss of situational awareness, or disorientation.

Skills: The applicant exhibits the skill to:

AA.IV.C.S1   Use proper techniques, checklists, and procedures to enter into, operate within, and recover from specific flight situations, as applicable.

Area of Operation V. Stall Prevention

Task A. Partial Flap Configuration Stall Prevention

References: AC 61-67, AC 120-109; FAA-H-8083-2, FAA-H-8083-3, FAA-H-8083-25; FSB Report (type specific); POH/AFM

Objective: To determine the applicant exhibits satisfactory knowledge, risk management, and skills associated with stalls in a partial flap configuration.

Note: See Appendix 2: Safety of Flight and Appendix 3: Aircraft, Equipment, and Operational Requirements & Limitations for information related to this Task.

Knowledge:	The applicant demonstrates understanding of:
AA.V.A.K1	Aerodynamics associated with stalls in a partial flap configuration, including the relationship between angle of attack, airspeed, load factor, power setting, aircraft weight and balance, aircraft attitude, and sideslip effects.
AA.V.A.K2	Stall characteristics as they relate to airplane design, and recognition impending stall and full stall indications using sight, sound, or feel.
AA.V.A.K3	Factors and situations that can lead to a stall during takeoff or while on approach and actions that can be taken to prevent it.
AA.V.A.K4	Effects of autoflight, flight envelope protection in normal and degraded modes, and unexpected disconnects of the autopilot or autothrottle/autothrust, if applicable to the aircraft used for the evaluation.
AA.V.A.K5	Fundamentals of stall recovery.

Risk Management:	The applicant is able to identify, assess, and mitigate risk associated with:
AA.V.A.R1	Factors and situations that could lead to an inadvertent stall, spin, and loss of control during takeoff or while on approach.
AA.V.A.R2	Range and limitations of stall warning indicators (e.g., aircraft buffet, stall horn, stick shaker, etc.).
AA.V.A.R3	Stall warning awareness.
AA.V.A.R4	Stall recovery procedure.
AA.V.A.R5	Secondary stalls, accelerated stalls, elevator trim stalls, and cross-control stalls.
AA.V.A.R6	Effect of environmental elements on aircraft performance while in a partial flap configuration as it relates to stalls (e.g., turbulence, microbursts, and high-density altitude).
AA.V.A.R7	Collision hazards including aircraft and terrain.
AA.V.A.R8	Distractions, task prioritization, loss of situational awareness, or disorientation.

Skills:	The applicant exhibits the skill to:
AA.V.A.S1	Clear the area and select an entry altitude that allows the recovery to be completed no lower than 3,000 feet above ground level (AGL) (non-transport category airplanes) or 5,000 feet AGL (transport category airplanes).
AA.V.A.S2	[Archived]
AA.V.A.S3	Establish the takeoff or approach configuration (partial flap), as specified by the evaluator, and maintain coordinated flight in simulated or actual instrument conditions throughout the maneuver.

AA.V.A.S4	Either manually or with the autopilot engaged, smoothly adjust pitch attitude, bank angle (15°-30°), and power setting in accordance with evaluator's instructions to an impending stall.
AA.V.A.S5	Acknowledge the cue(s) and promptly recover at the first indication of an impending stall (e.g., buffet, stall horn, stick shaker, etc.).
AA.V.A.S6	Execute a stall recovery in accordance with procedures set forth in the Pilot's Operating Handbook (POH)/Flight Manual (FM).
AA.V.A.S7	Retract the flaps or other lift/drag devices to the recommended setting, if applicable; retract the landing gear after a positive rate of climb is established, if applicable; and return to the desired flight path as specified by the evaluator.

Task B. Clean Configuration Stall Prevention

References: AC 61-67, AC 120-109; FAA-H-8083-2, FAA-H-8083-3, FAA-H-8083-25; FSB Report (type specific); POH/AFM

Objective: To determine the applicant exhibits satisfactory knowledge, risk management, and skills associated with stalls in a clean configuration.

Note: See Appendix 2: Safety of Flight and Appendix 3: Aircraft, Equipment, and Operational Requirements & Limitations for information related to this Task.

Knowledge:	The applicant demonstrates understanding of:
AA.V.B.K1	Aerodynamics associated with stalls in a clean configuration, including the relationship between angle of attack, airspeed, load factor, power setting, aircraft weight and balance, and aircraft attitude.
AA.V.B.K2	Stall characteristics as they relate to airplane design, and recognition impending stall and full stall indications using sight, sound, or feel.
AA.V.B.K3	Factors and situations that can lead to a stall during cruise flight and actions that can be taken to prevent it.
AA.V.B.K4	Effects of autoflight, flight envelope protection in normal and degraded modes, and unexpected disconnects of the autopilot or autothrottle/autothrust, if applicable to the aircraft used for the evaluation.
AA.V.B.K5	Fundamentals of stall recovery.
AA.V.B.K6	Effects of altitude on performance (e.g., thrust available) and flight control effectiveness during a recovery.

Risk Management:	The applicant is able to identify, assess, and mitigate risk associated with:
AA.V.B.R1	Factors and situations that could lead to an inadvertent stall, spin, and loss of control during cruise flight.
AA.V.B.R2	Range and limitations of stall warning indicators (e.g., aircraft buffet, stall horn, stick shaker, etc.).
AA.V.B.R3	Stall warning awareness.
AA.V.B.R4	Stall recovery procedure.
AA.V.B.R5	Secondary stalls, accelerated stalls, elevator trim stalls, and cross-control stalls.
AA.V.B.R6	Effect of environmental elements on aircraft performance while in cruise flight as it relates to stalls (e.g., turbulence, microbursts, and high-density altitude).

| AA.V.B.R7 | Collision hazards including aircraft and terrain. |

| AA.V.B.R8 | Distractions, task prioritization, loss of situational awareness, or disorientation. |

Skills:	The applicant exhibits the skill to:
AA.V.B.S1	Clear the area and select an entry altitude that allows the recovery to be completed no lower than 3,000 feet above ground level (AGL) (non-transport category airplanes) or 5,000 feet AGL (transport category airplanes).
AA.V.B.S2	[Archived]
AA.V.B.S3	While in cruise flight, maintain coordinated flight in simulated or actual instrument conditions throughout the maneuver.
AA.V.B.S4	Either manually or with the autopilot engaged, smoothly adjust pitch attitude, bank angle (15°-30°), and power setting in accordance with evaluator's instructions to an impending stall.
AA.V.B.S5	Acknowledge the cue(s) and promptly recover at the first indication of an impending stall (e.g., buffet, stall horn, stick shaker, etc.).
AA.V.B.S6	Execute a stall recovery in accordance with procedures set forth in the Pilot's Operating Handbook (POH)/Flight Manual (FM).
AA.V.B.S7	Return to the desired flight path as specified by the evaluator.

Task C. Landing Configuration Stall Prevention

References: AC 61-67, AC 120-109; FAA-H-8083-2, FAA-H-8083-3, FAA-H-8083-25; FSB Report (type specific); POH/AFM

Objective: To determine the applicant exhibits satisfactory knowledge, risk management, and skills associated with stalls in the landing configuration

Note: See Appendix 2: Safety of Flight and Appendix 3: Aircraft, Equipment, and Operational Requirements & Limitations for information related to this Task.

Knowledge:	The applicant demonstrates understanding of:
AA.V.C.K1	Aerodynamics associated with stalls in the landing configuration, including the relationship between angle of attack, airspeed, load factor, power setting, aircraft weight and balance, aircraft attitude, and sideslip effects.
AA.V.C.K2	Stall characteristics as they relate to airplane design, and recognition impending stall and full stall indications using sight, sound, or feel.
AA.V.C.K3	Factors and situations that can lead to a stall when configured for landing and actions that can be taken to prevent it.
AA.V.C.K4	Effects of autoflight, flight envelope protection in normal and degraded modes, and unexpected disconnects of the autopilot or autothrottle/autothrust, if applicable to the aircraft used for the evaluation.
AA.V.C.K5	Fundamentals of stall recovery.

Risk Management:	The applicant is able to identify, assess, and mitigate risk associated with:
AA.V.C.R1	Factors and situations that could lead to an inadvertent stall, spin, and loss of control during landing.
AA.V.C.R2	Range and limitations of stall warning indicators (e.g., aircraft buffet, stall horn, stick shaker, etc.).

AA.V.C.R3   Stall warning awareness.

AA.V.C.R4   Stall recovery procedure.

AA.V.C.R5   Secondary stalls, accelerated stalls, elevator trim stalls, and cross-control stalls.

AA.V.C.R6   Effect of environmental elements on aircraft performance while landing as it relates to stalls (e.g., turbulence, icing, microbursts, and high-density altitude).

AA.V.C.R7   Stalls at a low altitude.

AA.V.C.R8   Collision hazards, including aircraft and terrain.

AA.V.C.R9   Distractions, task prioritization, loss of situational awareness, or disorientation.

Skills:	The applicant exhibits the skill to:

AA.V.C.S1   Clear the area and select an entry altitude that allows the recovery to be completed no lower than 3,000 feet above ground level (AGL) (non-transport category airplanes) or 5,000 feet AGL (transport category airplanes).

AA.V.C.S2   [Archived]

AA.V.C.S3   Establish the landing configuration (i.e., lift/drag devices set and landing gear extended) and maintain coordinated flight in simulated or actual instrument conditions throughout the maneuver.

AA.V.C.S4   Either manually or with the autopilot engaged, smoothly adjust pitch attitude, bank angle (15°-30°), and power setting in accordance with evaluator's instructions to an impending stall.

AA.V.C.S5   Acknowledge the cue(s) and promptly recover at the first indication of an impending stall (e.g., buffet, stall horn, stick shaker, etc.).

AA.V.C.S6   Execute a stall recovery in accordance with procedures set forth in the Pilot's Operating Handbook (POH)/Flight Manual (FM).

AA.V.C.S7   Retract the flaps or other lift/drag devices to the recommended setting, if applicable; retract the landing gear after a positive rate of climb is established, if applicable; and return to the desired flight path as specified by the evaluator.

Area of Operation VI. Instrument Procedures

Task A. Instrument Takeoff

References: *14 CFR part 91; AIM; FAA-H-8083-2, FAA-H-8083-3, FAA-H-8083-15, FAA-H-8083-16, FAA-H-8083-23, FAA-H-8083-25; POH/AFM; Terminal Procedures Publications*

Objective: To determine the applicant exhibits satisfactory knowledge, risk management, and skills associated with an instrument takeoff.

Note: *See Appendix 3: Aircraft, Equipment, and Operational Requirements & Limitations for information related to this Task.*

Knowledge: The applicant demonstrates understanding of:

AA.VI.A.K1	Operational factors that could affect an instrument takeoff (e.g., runway length, runway lighting, surface conditions, wind, wake turbulence, icing conditions, obstructions, available instrument approaches or alternate airports available) in the event of an emergency after takeoff.

Risk Management: The applicant is able to identify, assess, and mitigate risk associated with:

AA.VI.A.R1	Selection of a runway based on aircraft performance and limitations, available distance, surface conditions, lighting, and wind.
AA.VI.A.R2	Wake turbulence.
AA.VI.A.R3	Abnormal operations, including planning for:
AA.VI.A.R3a	a. Rejected takeoff
AA.VI.A.R3b	b. Potential engine failure in takeoff/climb phase of flight with the ceiling or visibility below the minimums for an instrument approach at departure airport
AA.VI.A.R4	Collision hazards.
AA.VI.A.R5	Low altitude maneuvering, including stall, spin, or controlled flight into terrain (CFIT).
AA.VI.A.R6	Distractions, task prioritization, loss of situational awareness, or disorientation.

Skills: The applicant exhibits the skill to:

AA.VI.A.S1	Coordinate with crew, if applicable, and complete the appropriate checklist(s) prior to takeoff in a timely manner.
AA.VI.A.S2	Properly set the applicable avionics and flight instruments prior to initiating the takeoff.
AA.VI.A.S3	Make radio calls as appropriate.
AA.VI.A.S4	Verify assigned/correct runway (ASEL, AMEL) or takeoff path (ASES, AMES).
AA.VI.A.S5	Position the flight controls for the existing wind, if applicable.
AA.VI.A.S6	Clear the area, taxi into takeoff position, and align the airplane on the runway centerline (ASEL, AMEL) or takeoff path (ASES, AMES).
AA.VI.A.S7	Perform an instrument takeoff with instrument meteorological conditions (IMC) simulated at or before reaching an altitude of 100 feet above ground level (AGL). If accomplished in a full flight simulator, visibility should be no greater than ¼ mile, or as specified by applicable operations specifications, whichever is lower.
AA.VI.A.S8	Maintain centerline (ASEL, AMEL) and proper flight control inputs during the takeoff roll.
AA.VI.A.S9	Confirm takeoff power and proper engine and flight instrument indications prior to rotation making callouts, as appropriate, for the airplane or per the operator's procedures.

AA.VI.A.S10	Rotate and lift off at the recommended airspeed, establish the desired pitch attitude, and accelerate to the desired airspeed/V-speed.
AA.VI.A.S11	Transition smoothly from visual meteorological conditions (VMC) to actual or simulated instrument meteorological conditions (IMC).
AA.VI.A.S12	Maintain desired heading ±5° and desired airspeeds ±5 knots.
AA.VI.A.S13	Comply with air traffic control (ATC) clearances and instructions issued by ATC or the evaluator, as appropriate.
AA.VI.A.S14	Complete appropriate after takeoff checklist(s) in a timely manner.

Task B. Departure Procedures

References: *14 CFR part 91; AC 90-100; AIM; FAA-H-8083-2, FAA-H-8083-3, FAA-H-8083-15, FAA-H-8083-16, FAA-H-8083-25; POH/AFM; Terminal Procedures Publications*

Objective: To determine the applicant exhibits satisfactory knowledge, risk management, and skills associated with instrument departure procedures (DPs).

Note: *See Appendix 3: Aircraft, Equipment, and Operational Requirements & Limitations for information related to this Task.*

Knowledge:	The applicant demonstrates understanding of:
AA.VI.B.K1	Takeoff minimums; (Obstacle) Departure Procedure (ODP), including Visual Climb over the Airport (VCOA) and Diverse Vector Area (Radar Vectors); Standard Instrument Departure (SID), including Area Navigation (RNAV) departure; required climb gradients; U.S. Terminal Procedures Publications; and En Route Charts.
AA.VI.B.K2	Use of a Flight Management System (FMS) or Global Positioning System (GPS) to follow a DP.
AA.VI.B.K3	Pilot/controller responsibilities, communication procedures, and ATC services available to pilots.
AA.VI.B.K4	Two-way radio communication failure procedures after takeoff.
AA.VI.B.K5	Ground-based and satellite-based navigation systems (orientation, course determination, equipment, tests and regulations, interference, appropriate use of navigation data, signal integrity).

Risk Management:	The applicant is able to identify, assess, and mitigate risk associated with:
AA.VI.B.R1	Following published procedures and required climb gradients or ATC Instructions.
AA.VI.B.R2	Limitations of air traffic avoidance equipment and use of see and avoid techniques.
AA.VI.B.R3	Automation management.

Skills:	The applicant exhibits the skill to:
AA.VI.B.S1	Select the appropriate instrument departure procedure. Then select, identify (as necessary), and use the appropriate communication and navigation facilities associated with the procedure.
AA.VI.B.S2	Program the FMS prior to departure and set avionics, including flight director and autopilot controls, as appropriate, for the departure, if applicable.
AA.VI.B.S3	Coordinate with crew, if applicable, and complete the appropriate checklist(s) in a timely manner.
AA.VI.B.S4	Use current and appropriate navigation publications or databases for the proposed flight.
AA.VI.B.S5	Establish two-way communications with the proper controlling agency, use proper phraseology, comply, in a timely manner, with all ATC instructions and airspace restrictions, and exhibit adequate knowledge of communication failure procedures.

AA.VI.B.S6	Intercept all courses, radials, and bearings appropriate to the procedure, route, clearance, or as directed by the evaluator in a timely manner.
AA.VI.B.S7	Comply with all applicable charted procedures.
AA.VI.B.S8	Maintain the appropriate airspeed ±10 knots, headings ±10°, and altitude ±100 feet, and accurately track a course, radial, or bearing.
AA.VI.B.S9	Conduct the departure phase to a point where, in the opinion of the evaluator, the transition to the en route environment is complete.

Task C. Arrival Procedures

References: 14 CFR part 91; AC 90-100; AIM; FAA-H-8083-2, FAA-H-8083-3, FAA-H-8083-15, FAA-H-8083-16, FAA-H-8083-25; IFR Enroute Charts; POH/AFM; STARs; Terminal Procedures Publications

Objective: To determine the applicant exhibits satisfactory knowledge, risk management, and skills associated with Instrument Flight Rules (IFR) arrival procedures.

Note: See Appendix 3: Aircraft, Equipment, and Operational Requirements & Limitations for information related to this Task.

Knowledge:	The applicant demonstrates understanding of:
AA.VI.C.K1	Standard Terminal Arrival (STAR) charts, U.S. Terminal Procedures Publications, and IFR En Route High and Low Altitude Charts.
AA.VI.C.K2	Use of a Flight Management System (FMS) or GPS to follow a STAR.
AA.VI.C.K3	Pilot/controller responsibilities, communication procedures, and ATC services available to pilots.
AA.VI.C.K4	Two-way radio communication failure procedures during an arrival.
AA.VI.C.K5	Ground-based and satellite-based navigation systems (orientation, course determination, equipment, tests and regulations, interference, appropriate use of navigation data, signal integrity).

Risk Management:	The applicant is able to identify, assess, and mitigate risk associated with:
AA.VI.C.R1	ATC communications and compliance with published procedures.
AA.VI.C.R2	Limitations of traffic avoidance equipment.
AA.VI.C.R3	Responsibility to use "see and avoid" techniques when possible.
AA.VI.C.R4	Automation management.
AA.VI.C.R5	ATC instructions that modify an arrival or discontinue/resume the aircraft's lateral or vertical navigation on an arrival.

Skills:	The applicant exhibits the skill to:
AA.VI.C.S1	In actual or simulated instrument conditions, select, identify (as necessary) and use the appropriate communication and navigation facilities associated with the arrival.
AA.VI.C.S2	Set FMS and avionics, including flight director and autopilot controls for the arrival, if applicable.
AA.VI.C.S3	Coordinate with crew, if applicable, and complete the appropriate checklist(s) in a timely manner.
AA.VI.C.S4	Use current and appropriate navigation publications or databases for the proposed flight.
AA.VI.C.S5	Establish two-way communications with the proper controlling agency, use proper phraseology and comply, in a timely manner, with all ATC instructions and airspace restrictions as well as exhibit adequate knowledge of communication failure procedures.

AA.VI.C.S6	Intercept all courses, radials, and bearings appropriate to the procedure, route, clearance, or as directed by the evaluator in a timely manner.
AA.VI.C.S7	Comply with all applicable charted procedures.
AA.VI.C.S8	Adhere to airspeed restrictions required by regulation, procedure, aircraft limitation, ATC, or the evaluator.
AA.VI.C.S9	Establish rates of descent consistent with the route segment, airplane operating characteristics and safety.
AA.VI.C.S10	Maintain the appropriate airspeed/V-speed ±10 knots, but not less than reference landing approach speed (V_{REF}) if applicable, heading ±10°, altitude ±100 feet, and accurately track radials, courses, and bearings.

Task D. Non-precision Approaches

References: *14 CFR part 91; AC 120-108; AIM; Chart Supplements; FAA-H-8083-2, FAA-H-8083-3, FAA-H-8083-15, FAA-H-8083-16, FAA-H-8083-25; Terminal Procedures Publications*

Objective: To determine the applicant exhibits satisfactory knowledge, risk management, and skills associated with performing non-precision approach procedures.

Note: *See Appendix 3: Aircraft, Equipment, and Operational Requirements & Limitations for information related to this Task.*

Knowledge:	The applicant demonstrates understanding of:
AA.VI.D.K1	Procedures and limitations associated with a non-precision approach, including the differences between Localizer Performance (LP) and Lateral Navigation (LNAV) approach guidance.
AA.VI.D.K2	Navigation system displays and annunciations, modes of operation, and Required Navigation Performance (RNP) lateral accuracy values associated with an RNAV (GPS) approach.
AA.VI.D.K3	Ground-based and satellite-based navigation systems (orientation, course determination, equipment, tests and regulations, interference, appropriate use of navigation data, signal integrity).
AA.VI.D.K4	A stabilized approach, including energy management concepts.

Risk Management:	The applicant is able to identify, assess, and mitigate risk associated with:
AA.VI.D.R1	Deviating from the assigned approach procedure.
AA.VI.D.R2	Selecting a navigation frequency.
AA.VI.D.R3	Management of automated navigation and autoflight systems.
AA.VI.D.R4	Aircraft configuration during an approach and missed approach.
AA.VI.D.R5	An unstable approach, including excessive descent rates.
AA.VI.D.R6	Deteriorating weather conditions on approach.
AA.VI.D.R7	Operating below the minimum descent altitude (MDA) without proper visual references.

Skills:	The applicant exhibits the skill to:
AA.VI.D.S1	Accomplish the non-precision instrument approaches selected by the evaluator.
AA.VI.D.S2	Establish two-way communications with air traffic control (ATC) appropriate for the phase of flight or approach segment, and use proper communication phraseology.
AA.VI.D.S3	Select, tune, identify, and confirm the operational status of navigation equipment to be used for the approach.

AA.VI.D.S4	Comply with all clearances issued by ATC or the evaluator.
AA.VI.D.S5	Recognize if any flight instrumentation is inaccurate or inoperative, and take appropriate action.
AA.VI.D.S6	Advise ATC or the evaluator if unable to comply with a clearance.
AA.VI.D.S7	Coordinate with crew, if applicable, and complete the appropriate checklist(s) in a timely manner.
AA.VI.D.S8	Establish the appropriate airplane configuration and airspeed considering meteorological and operating conditions.
AA.VI.D.S9	Maintain altitude ±100 feet, selected heading ±5°, airspeed ±10 knots, and accurately track radials, courses, and bearings, prior to beginning the final approach segment.
AA.VI.D.S10	Adjust the published MDA/Derived Decision Altitude (DDA) and visibility criteria for the aircraft approach category, as appropriate, for factors that include Notices to Air Missions (NOTAMs), inoperative aircraft or navigation equipment, or inoperative visual aids associated with the landing environment, etc.
AA.VI.D.S11	Establish a stabilized descent to the appropriate altitude.
AA.VI.D.S12	For the final approach segment, maintain no more than ¼ scale course deviation indicator (CDI) deflection, airspeed ±5 knots of selected value, and altitude above MDA +50/-0 feet [to the visual descent point (VDP) or missed approach point (MAP)].
AA.VI.D.S13	Execute the missed approach procedure if the required visual references are not distinctly visible and identifiable at the appropriate point or altitude for the approach profile; or execute a normal landing from a straight-in or circling approach.
AA.VI.D.S14	Use a Multi-Function Display (MFD) and other graphical navigation displays, if installed, to monitor position, track wind drift and other parameters to maintain desired flightpath.

Task E. Precision Approaches

References: *14 CFR parts 91, 97; AIM; Chart Supplements; FAA-H-8083-2, FAA-H-8083-3, FAA-H-8083-15, FAA-H-8083-16, FAA-H-8083-25; Terminal Procedures Publications*

Objective: To determine the applicant exhibits satisfactory knowledge, risk management, and skills associated with performing precision approach procedures.

Note: *See Appendix 3: Aircraft, Equipment, and Operational Requirements & Limitations for information related to this Task.*

Knowledge: The applicant demonstrates understanding of:

AA.VI.E.K1	Procedures and limitations associated with a precision approach, including determining required descent rates and adjusting minimums in the case of inoperative equipment.
AA.VI.E.K2	Navigation system displays, annunciations, and modes of operation.
AA.VI.E.K3	Ground-based and satellite-based navigation systems (orientation, course determination, equipment, tests and regulations, interference, appropriate use of navigation data, signal integrity).
AA.VI.E.K4	A stabilized approach, including energy management concepts.

Risk Management: The applicant is able to identify, assess, and mitigate risk associated with:

AA.VI.E.R1	Deviating from the assigned approach procedure.
AA.VI.E.R2	Selecting a navigation frequency.
AA.VI.E.R3	Management of automated navigation and autoflight systems.
AA.VI.E.R4	Aircraft configuration during an approach and missed approach.

AA.VI.E.R5	An unstable approach, including excessive descent rates.
AA.VI.E.R6	Deteriorating weather conditions on approach.
AA.VI.E.R7	Continuing to descend below the Decision Altitude (DA)/Decision Height (DH) when the required visual references are not visible.

Skills:	The applicant exhibits the skill to:
AA.VI.E.S1	Accomplish the precision instrument approaches selected by the evaluator.
AA.VI.E.S2	Establish two-way communications with air traffic control (ATC) appropriate for the phase of flight or approach segment, and use proper communication phraseology.
AA.VI.E.S3	Select, tune, identify, and confirm the operational status of navigation equipment to be used for the approach.
AA.VI.E.S4	Comply in a timely manner with all clearances, instructions, and procedures.
AA.VI.E.S5	Recognize if any flight instrumentation is inaccurate or inoperative, and take appropriate action.
AA.VI.E.S6	Advise ATC or the evaluator if unable to comply with a clearance.
AA.VI.E.S7	Coordinate with crew, if applicable, and complete the appropriate checklist(s) in a timely manner.
AA.VI.E.S8	Establish the appropriate airplane configuration and airspeed considering meteorological and operating conditions.
AA.VI.E.S9	Maintain altitude ±100 feet, selected heading ±5°, airspeed ±10 knots, and accurately track radials, courses, and bearings, prior to beginning the final approach segment.
AA.VI.E.S10	Adjust the published DA/DH and visibility criteria for the aircraft approach category, as appropriate, to account for NOTAMS, inoperative airplane or navigation equipment, or inoperative visual aids associated with the landing environment.
AA.VI.E.S11	Establish a predetermined rate of descent at the point where vertical guidance begins, which approximates that required for the aircraft to follow the vertical guidance.
AA.VI.E.S12	Maintain a stabilized final approach from the Final Approach Fix (FAF) to DA/DH allowing no more than ¼-scale deflection of either the vertical or lateral guidance indications and maintain the desired airspeed ±5 knots.
AA.VI.E.S13	Upon reaching the DA/DH, immediately initiate the missed approach procedures if the required visual references for the runway are not distinctly visible and identifiable (or if in a seaplane); or transition to a normal landing approach only when the aircraft is in a position from which a descent to a landing on the runway can be made at a normal rate of descent using normal maneuvering.
AA.VI.E.S14	Use an MFD and other graphical navigation displays, if installed, to monitor position, track wind drift and other parameters to maintain desired flightpath.

Task F. Landing from a Precision Approach

References: 14 CFR part 91; AIM; FAA-H-8083-2, FAA-H-8083-3, FAA-H-8083-15, FAA-H-8083-16, FAA-H-8083-25; SAFO 19001

Objective: To determine the applicant exhibits satisfactory knowledge, risk management, and skills associated with performing the procedures for a landing from a precision approach.

Note: See Appendix 3: Aircraft, Equipment, and Operational Requirements & Limitations for information related to this Task.

Note: For non-amphibious seaplanes, this task applies only when the applicant has immediate access to an instrument approach to a waterway.

Knowledge: The applicant demonstrates understanding of:

AA.VI.F.K1 Elements related to the pilot's responsibilities, and the environmental, operational, and meteorological factors that affect landing from a precision approach.

AA.VI.F.K2 Approach lighting systems and runway and taxiway signs, markings, and lighting.

Risk Management: The applicant is able to identify, assess, and mitigate risk associated with:

AA.VI.F.R1 Selection of an approach procedure and runway based on aircraft limitations, available distance, surface conditions, and wind.

AA.VI.F.R2 Wake turbulence.

AA.VI.F.R3 [Archived]

AA.VI.F.R3a a. [Archived]

AA.VI.F.R3b b. [Archived]

AA.VI.F.R4 Collision hazards.

AA.VI.F.R5 Low altitude maneuvering, including stall, spin, or controlled flight into terrain (CFIT).

AA.VI.F.R6 Distractions, task prioritization, loss of situational awareness, or disorientation.

AA.VI.F.R7 Attempting to land from an unstable approach.

AA.VI.F.R8 Flying below the glidepath.

AA.VI.F.R9 Transitioning from instrument to visual references for landing.

AA.VI.F.R10 Missed Approach.

AA.VI.F.R11 Land and hold short operations (LAHSO).

Skills: The applicant exhibits the skill to:

AA.VI.F.S1 Maintain the desired airspeed, ±5 knots, and vertical and lateral guidance within ¼-scale deflection of the indicators during the descent from DA/DH to a point where visual maneuvering is used to accomplish a normal landing.

AA.VI.F.S2 Adhere to all ATC or evaluator advisories, such as NOTAMs, windshear, wake turbulence, runway surface, braking conditions, and other operational considerations.

AA.VI.F.S3 Coordinate with crew, if applicable, and complete the appropriate checklist(s) in a timely manner.

AA.VI.F.S4 Touch down at the aiming point markings, -250/+500 feet, or where there are no runway aiming point markings, 750 to 1,500 feet, from the approach threshold of the runway.

AA.VI.F.S5 Maintain positive airplane control throughout the landing using drag and braking devices, as appropriate, to come to a stop.

AA.VI.F.S6 Use single-pilot resource management (SRM) or crew resource management (CRM), as appropriate.

AA.VI.F.S7 Use runway incursion avoidance procedures, if applicable.

Task G. Circling Approach

References: *14 CFR parts 91, 97; AIM; Chart Supplements; FAA-H-8083-2, FAA-H-8083-3, FAA-H-8083-15, FAA-H-8083-16, FAA-H-8083-25; Terminal Procedures Publications*

Objective: To determine the applicant exhibits satisfactory knowledge, risk management, and skills associated with performing a circling approach procedure.

Note: *See Appendix 3: Aircraft, Equipment, and Operational Requirements & Limitations for information related to this Task.*

Knowledge:	The applicant demonstrates understanding of:
AA.VI.G.K1	Elements related to circling approach procedures and limitations, including approach categories and related airspeed restrictions.

Risk Management:	The applicant is able to identify, assess, and mitigate risk associated with:
AA.VI.G.R1	Prescribed circling approach procedures.
AA.VI.G.R2	Executing a circling approach at night or with marginal visibility.
AA.VI.G.R3	Losing visual contact with an identifiable part of the airport.
AA.VI.G.R4	Management of automated navigation and autoflight systems.
AA.VI.G.R5	Control of altitude, airspeed, and distance while circling.
AA.VI.G.R6	Low altitude maneuvering, including stall, spin, or controlled flight into terrain (CFIT).
AA.VI.G.R7	Executing a missed approach after the MAP while circling.

Skills:	The applicant exhibits the skill to:
AA.VI.G.S1	Comply with the circling approach procedure considering turbulence, windshear, and the maneuvering capability and approach category of the aircraft.
AA.VI.G.S2	Confirm the direction of traffic and adhere to all restrictions and instructions issued by ATC or the evaluator.
AA.VI.G.S3	Coordinate with crew, if applicable, and complete the appropriate checklist(s) in a timely manner.
AA.VI.G.S4	Establish the approach and landing configuration. Maintain a stabilized approach and a descent rate that ensures arrival at the MDA, or the preselected circling altitude above the MDA, prior to the missed approach point.
AA.VI.G.S5	Maintain airspeed ±5 knots, desired heading/track ±5°, and altitude +100/-0 feet until descending below the MDA or the preselected circling altitude above the MDA.
AA.VI.G.S6	Visually maneuver to a base or downwind leg appropriate for the landing runway and environmental conditions.
AA.VI.G.S7	If a missed approach occurs, turn in the appropriate direction using the correct procedure and appropriately configure the airplane.

Task H. Landing from a Circling Approach

References: *14 CFR part 91; AIM; FAA-H-8083-2, FAA-H-8083-3, FAA-H-8083-15, FAA-H-8083-16, FAA-H-8083-25; SAFO 19001*

Objective: To determine the applicant exhibits satisfactory knowledge, risk management, and skills associated with performing the procedures for a landing from a circling approach.

Knowledge:	The applicant demonstrates understanding of:
AA.VI.H.K1	Elements related to the pilot's responsibilities, and the environmental, operational, and meteorological factors that affect landing from a circling approach.
AA.VI.H.K2	Approach lighting systems and runway and taxiway signs, markings, and lighting.

Risk Management:	The applicant is able to identify, assess, and mitigate risk associated with:
AA.VI.H.R1	Selection of an approach procedure and runway based on aircraft limitations, available distance, surface conditions, and wind.
AA.VI.H.R2	Wake turbulence.
AA.VI.H.R3	[Archived]
AA.VI.H.R3a	a. [Archived]
AA.VI.H.R3b	b. [Archived]
AA.VI.H.R4	Collision hazards.
AA.VI.H.R5	Low altitude maneuvering, including stall, spin, or controlled flight into terrain (CFIT).
AA.VI.H.R6	Distractions, task prioritization, loss of situational awareness, or disorientation.
AA.VI.H.R7	Attempting to land from an unstable approach.
AA.VI.H.R8	Missed Approach.
AA.VI.H.R9	Land and hold short operations (LAHSO).

Skills:	The applicant exhibits the skill to:
AA.VI.H.S1	Keep the airport environment in sight and remain within the circling approach radius applicable to the approach category to a position from which a stabilized descent to landing can be made.
AA.VI.H.S2	Adhere to all ATC or evaluator advisories, such as NOTAMs, windshear, wake turbulence, runway surface, braking conditions, and other operational considerations.
AA.VI.H.S3	Coordinate with crew, if applicable, and complete the appropriate checklist(s) in a timely manner.
AA.VI.H.S4	Aligns the airplane for a normal landing on the selected runway without excessive maneuvering and without exceeding the normal operating limits of the airplane. The angle of bank should not exceed 30°.
AA.VI.H.S5	Make smooth, timely, and correct control application throughout the circling maneuver and maintain appropriate airspeed, ±5 knots. If applicable, maintain altitude +100/–0 feet, and desired heading/ track, ±5°.
AA.VI.H.S6	Ensure the airplane is configured for landing.
AA.VI.H.S7	Scan the landing runway and adjoining area for traffic and obstructions. (ASEL, AMEL).
AA.VI.H.S8	Touch down at the aiming point markings - 250/+500 feet, or where there are no runway aiming point markings 750 to 1,500 feet from the approach threshold of the runway.
AA.VI.H.S9	Maintain positive aircraft control throughout the landing using drag and braking devices, as appropriate, to come to a stop.
AA.VI.H.S10	Use single-pilot resource management (SRM) or crew resource management (CRM), as appropriate.
AA.VI.H.S11	Use runway incursion avoidance procedures, if applicable.

Task I. Missed Approaches

References: 14 CFR parts 91, 97; AIM; FAA-H-8083-2, FAA-H-8083-3, FAA-H-8083-15, FAA-H-8083-16, FAA-H-8083-25; Terminal Procedures Publications

Objective: To determine the applicant exhibits satisfactory knowledge, risk management, and skills associated with performing a missed approach procedure.

Note: See Appendix 3: Aircraft, Equipment, and Operational Requirements & Limitations for information related to this Task.

Knowledge:	The applicant demonstrates understanding of:
AA.VI.I.K1	Elements related to missed approach procedures, including reference to standby or backup instruments.
AA.VI.I.K2	Limitations associated with standard instrument approaches, including while using an FMS or autopilot, if equipped.

Risk Management:	The applicant is able to identify, assess, and mitigate risk associated with:
AA.VI.I.R1	Deviations from prescribed procedures or ATC instructions.
AA.VI.I.R2	Holding, diverting, or electing to fly the approach again.
AA.VI.I.R3	Aircraft configuration during an approach and missed approach.
AA.VI.I.R4	Factors that might lead to executing a missed approach procedure before the MAP or to a go-around below DA, DH, or MDA, as applicable.
AA.VI.I.R5	Management of automated navigation and autoflight systems.

Skills:	The applicant exhibits the skill to:
AA.VI.I.S1	Promptly initiate the missed approach procedure and report it to ATC.
AA.VI.I.S2	Apply the appropriate power setting for the flight condition and establish a pitch attitude necessary to obtain the desired performance.
AA.VI.I.S3	Retract the wing flaps/drag devices and landing gear, if appropriate, in the correct sequence and at a safe altitude, and establish a positive rate of climb and the appropriate airspeed/V-speed, ±5 knots.
AA.VI.I.S4	Coordinate with crew, if applicable, and complete the appropriate procedures and checklist(s) in a timely manner.
AA.VI.I.S5	Comply with the published or alternate missed approach procedure.
AA.VI.I.S6	Advise ATC or the evaluator if unable to comply with a clearance, restriction, or climb gradient.
AA.VI.I.S7	Maintain the heading, course, or bearing ±5°, and altitude(s) ±100 feet during the missed approach procedure.
AA.VI.I.S8	Use an MFD and other graphical navigation displays, if installed, to monitor position and track to help navigate the missed approach.
AA.VI.I.S9	Use single-pilot resource management (SRM) or crew resource management (CRM), as appropriate.
AA.VI.I.S10	Re-engage autopilot (if installed) at appropriate times during the missed approach procedure.
AA.VI.I.S11	Request ATC clearance to attempt another approach, proceed to the alternate airport, holding fix, or other clearance limit, as appropriate, or as directed by the evaluator.

Task J. Holding Procedures

References: *14 CFR part 91; AC 91-74; AIM; FAA-H-8083-2, FAA-H-8083-3, FAA-H-8083-15, FAA-H-8083-16, FAA-H-8083-25; POH/AFM; Terminal Procedures Publications*

Objective: To determine the applicant exhibits satisfactory knowledge, risk management, and skills associated with holding procedures.

Note: *See Appendix 3: Aircraft, Equipment, and Operational Requirements & Limitations for information related to this Task.*

Knowledge:	The applicant demonstrates understanding of:
AA.VI.J.K1	Elements related to holding procedures, including reporting criteria, appropriate speeds, and recommended entry procedures for standard, nonstandard, published, and non-published holding patterns.
AA.VI.J.K2	Determining holding endurance based upon factors, including an expect further clearance (EFC) time, fuel on board, fuel flow while holding, fuel required to destination and alternate, etc., as appropriate.
AA.VI.J.K3	When to declare minimum fuel or a fuel-related emergency.
AA.VI.J.K4	Use of automation for holding, including autopilot and flight management systems, if equipped.

Risk Management:	The applicant is able to identify, assess, and mitigate risk associated with:
AA.VI.J.R1	Recalculating fuel reserves if assigned an unanticipated expect further clearance (EFC) time.
AA.VI.J.R2	Scenarios and circumstances that could result in minimum fuel or the need to declare an emergency.
AA.VI.J.R3	Scenarios that could lead to holding, including deteriorating weather at the planned destination.
AA.VI.J.R4	Holding entry and wind correction while holding.
AA.VI.J.R5	Holding while in icing conditions.
AA.VI.J.R6	Automation management.

Skills:	The applicant exhibits the skill to:
AA.VI.J.S1	Correctly identify instrument navigation aids associated with the assigned hold.
AA.VI.J.S2	Use an entry procedure appropriate for a standard, nonstandard, published, or non-published holding pattern.
AA.VI.J.S3	Change to the appropriate holding airspeed for the aircraft and holding altitude to cross the holding fix at or below maximum holding airspeed.
AA.VI.J.S4	Comply with the holding pattern leg length and other restrictions, if applicable, associated with the holding pattern.
AA.VI.J.S5	Comply with ATC reporting requirements.
AA.VI.J.S6	Use proper wind correction procedures to maintain the desired pattern and to arrive over the fix as close as possible to a specified time.
AA.VI.J.S7	Maintain specified airspeed ±10 knots, altitude ±100 feet, headings ±10°, and accurately track a selected course, radial, or bearing.
AA.VI.J.S8	If available, use automation, including autopilot, flight director controls, and navigation displays associated with the assigned hold.
AA.VI.J.S9	Update fuel reserve calculations based on EFC times.

Area of Operation VII. Emergency Operations

Task A. Emergency Procedures

References: *14 CFR part 91; AC 91-74; AIM; FAA-H-8083-2, FAA-H-8083-3, FAA-H-8083-23, FAA-H-8083-25; FSB Report (type specific); POH/AFM*

Objective: To determine the applicant exhibits satisfactory knowledge, risk management, and skills associated with emergency procedures.

Knowledge:	The applicant demonstrates understanding of:
AA.VII.A.K1	Declaring an emergency and selection of a suitable airport or landing location.
AA.VII.A.K2	Situations that would require an emergency descent (e.g., depressurization, smoke, or engine fire).
AA.VII.A.K3	Causes of inflight fire or smoke.
AA.VII.A.K4	Airplane decompression.
AA.VII.A.K5	When an emergency evacuation may be necessary.
AA.VII.A.K6	Actions required if icing conditions exceed the capabilities of the aircraft.

Risk Management:	The applicant is able to identify, assess, and mitigate risk associated with:
AA.VII.A.R1	Selection of the procedures or checklists to follow in an emergency.
AA.VII.A.R2	Multiple failures or system abnormalities.
AA.VII.A.R3	Altitude, wind, terrain, and obstruction considerations in an emergency.
AA.VII.A.R4	Distractions, task prioritization, loss of situational awareness, or disorientation.

Skills:	For the airplane provided for the practical test, the applicant demonstrates the ability to:
AA.VII.A.S1	Explain or describe an emergency procedure for a situation(s) presented by the evaluator.
AA.VII.A.S2	Use proper procedures for an emergency situation(s) presented by the evaluator, such as:
AA.VII.A.S2a	a. Emergency Descent
AA.VII.A.S2b	b. Inflight fire and smoke
AA.VII.A.S2c	c. Decompression
AA.VII.A.S2d	d. Emergency evacuation
AA.VII.A.S2e	e. Airframe icing
AA.VII.A.S2f	f. Others as specified in the Airplane Flight Manual (AFM)/Pilot's Operating Handbook (POH)
AA.VII.A.S3	Fly by reference to standby flight instruments, backup instrumentation, or partial panel, if applicable and appropriate to the situation.
AA.VII.A.S4	Coordinate with crew, if applicable, and complete the appropriate checklist(s) in a timely manner.
AA.VII.A.S5	Communicate with air traffic control (ATC) and the evaluator, as appropriate for the situation.

Task B. Powerplant Failure During Takeoff

References: FAA-H-8083-2, FAA-H-8083-3, FAA-H-8083-25; FSB Report (type specific); POH/AFM

Objective: To determine the applicant exhibits satisfactory knowledge, risk management, and skills associated with powerplant failure during takeoff.

Note: See Appendix 2: Safety of Flight and Appendix 3: Aircraft, Equipment, and Operational Requirements & Limitations for information related to this Task.

Knowledge:	The applicant demonstrates understanding of:
AA.VII.B.K1	The procedures used during a powerplant(s) failure on takeoff, the appropriate reference airspeeds, and the specific pilot actions required.
AA.VII.B.K2	Operational considerations, including: airplane performance (e.g., sideslip, bank angle, rudder input), takeoff warning systems, runway length, surface conditions, density altitude, wake turbulence, environmental conditions, obstructions, and other related factors that could adversely affect safety.

Risk Management:	The applicant is able to identify, assess, and mitigate risk associated with:
AA.VII.B.R1	Planning for a potential powerplant failure during takeoff considering operational factors (e.g., takeoff warning inhibit systems, other airplane characteristics, runway/takeoff path length, surface conditions, environmental conditions, obstructions, and land and hold short operations.
AA.VII.B.R2	Briefing the plan for a powerplant failure during takeoff, in a crew environment.
AA.VII.B.R3	Selection of the procedures or checklists to follow in an emergency.
AA.VII.B.R4	Identifying the inoperative engine (AMEL, AMES).
AA.VII.B.R5	Inability to climb or maintain altitude with an inoperative powerplant (AMEL, AMES).
AA.VII.B.R6	Altitude, wind, terrain, and obstruction considerations in an emergency.
AA.VII.B.R7	Low altitude maneuvering, including stall, spin, or controlled flight into terrain (CFIT).
AA.VII.B.R8	Distractions, task prioritization, loss of situational awareness, or disorientation.

Skills:	The applicant exhibits the skill to:
AA.VII.B.S1	Following the powerplant failure, maintain positive airplane control and adjust the powerplant controls as recommended by the manufacturer for the existing conditions.
AA.VII.B.S2	Establish a power-off descent approximately straight-ahead if the powerplant failure occurs after becoming airborne and before reaching an altitude where a safe turn can be made (ASEL, ASES) or the performance capabilities and operating limitations of the airplane do not allow the climb to continue (AMEL, AMES).
AA.VII.B.S3	Continue the takeoff if the (simulated) powerplant failure occurs at a point where the airplane can continue to a specified airspeed and altitude at the end of the runway commensurate with the airplane's performance capabilities and operating limitations (AMEL, AMES).
AA.VII.B.S4	After establishing a climb, maintain the desired airspeed, ±5 knots. Use flight controls in the proper combination as recommended by the manufacturer, or as required, to maintain best performance and trim as required (AMEL, AMES).
AA.VII.B.S5	Maintain the appropriate heading, ±5°, when powerplant failure occurs (AMEL, AMES).
AA.VII.B.S6	Coordinate with crew, if applicable, and complete the appropriate checklist(s) following the powerplant failure.
AA.VII.B.S7	Communicate with air traffic control (ATC) and the evaluator, as appropriate for the situation.

Task C. Powerplant Failure (Simulated) (ASEL, ASES)

References: FAA-H-8083-2, FAA-H-8083-3, FAA-H-8083-25; POH/AFM

Objective: To determine the applicant exhibits satisfactory knowledge, risk management, and skills associated with powerplant failure and associated emergency approach and landing procedures.

Note: See Appendix 2: Safety of Flight and Appendix 3: Aircraft, Equipment, and Operational Requirements & Limitations for information related to this Task.

Knowledge:	The applicant demonstrates understanding of:
AA.VII.C.K1	Immediate action items and emergency procedures for a forced landing.
AA.VII.C.K2	Airspeed, including:
AA.VII.C.K2a	a. Importance of best glide speed and its relationship to distance
AA.VII.C.K2b	b. Difference between best glide speed and minimum sink speed
AA.VII.C.K2c	c. Effects of wind on glide distance
AA.VII.C.K3	Effects of atmospheric conditions on emergency approach and landing.
AA.VII.C.K4	A stabilized approach, including energy management concepts.
AA.VII.C.K5	Emergency Locator Transmitters (ELTs) and other emergency locating devices.
AA.VII.C.K6	Air traffic control (ATC) services to aircraft in distress.

Risk Management:	The applicant is able to identify, assess, and mitigate risk associated with:
AA.VII.C.R1	Altitude, wind, terrain, obstructions, gliding distance, and available landing distance considerations.
AA.VII.C.R2	Following or changing the planned flightpath to the selected landing area.
AA.VII.C.R3	Collision hazards.
AA.VII.C.R4	Configuring the airplane.
AA.VII.C.R5	Low altitude maneuvering, including stall, spin, or controlled flight into terrain (CFIT).
AA.VII.C.R6	Distractions, task prioritization, loss of situational awareness, or disorientation.
AA.VII.C.R7	A powerplant failure in Instrument Meteorological Conditions (IMC).

Skills:	The applicant exhibits the skill to:
AA.VII.C.S1	Recognize the powerplant failure.
AA.VII.C.S2	Determine the cause for the simulated powerplant failure (if altitude permits) and if a restart is a viable option.
AA.VII.C.S3	Maintain positive control throughout the maneuver.
AA.VII.C.S4	Establish and maintain the recommended best glide airspeed, ±5 knots.
AA.VII.C.S5	Configure the airplane in accordance with the Pilot's Operating Handbook (POH)\Airplane Flight Manual (AFM) and existing conditions.
AA.VII.C.S6	Select a suitable landing area considering altitude, wind, terrain, obstructions, and available glide distance.
AA.VII.C.S7	Establish a proper flight path to the selected landing area.
AA.VII.C.S8	Complete emergency checklist items appropriate to the airplane in a timely manner and as recommended by the manufacturer or operator.

AA.VII.C.S9   Communicate with air traffic control (ATC) and the evaluator, as appropriate for the situation.

Task D. Inflight Powerplant(s) Failure and Restart (AMEL, AMES)

References: FAA-H-8083-2, FAA-H-8083-3, FAA-H-8083-25; POH/AFM

Objective: To determine the applicant exhibits satisfactory knowledge, risk management, and skills associated with inflight powerplant failure and restart procedures, if applicable, in a multiengine airplane.

Note: See Appendix 2: Safety of Flight and Appendix 3: Aircraft, Equipment, and Operational Requirements & Limitations for information related to this Task.

Knowledge:	The applicant demonstrates understanding of:
AA.VII.D.K1	Flight characteristics and controllability associated with maneuvering the airplane with powerplant(s) inoperative, including the importance of drag reduction.
AA.VII.D.K2	Powerplant restart procedures and conditions where a restart attempt is appropriate.

Risk Management:	The applicant is able to identify, assess, and mitigate risk associated with:
AA.VII.D.R1	Powerplant(s) failure.
AA.VII.D.R2	Methods for handling a powerplant failure or a powerplant restart.
AA.VII.D.R3	Diagnosis of the cause of the powerplant failure.
AA.VII.D.R4	Collision hazards.
AA.VII.D.R5	Configuring the airplane.
AA.VII.D.R6	Factors and situations that could lead to an inadvertent stall, spin, and loss of control with an inflight powerplant failure.
AA.VII.D.R7	Distractions, task prioritization, loss of situational awareness, or disorientation.

Skills:	The applicant exhibits the skill to:
AA.VII.D.S1	Recognize and correctly identify powerplant(s) failure, complete memory items (if applicable), and maintain positive airplane control.
AA.VII.D.S2	Coordinate with crew, if applicable, and complete the appropriate emergency procedures and checklist(s) for propeller feathering or powerplant shutdown.
AA.VII.D.S3	Use flight controls in the proper combination as recommended by the manufacturer, or as required to maintain best performance, and trim as required.
AA.VII.D.S4	Determine the cause for the powerplant(s) failure and if a restart is a viable option.
AA.VII.D.S5	Maintain the operating powerplant(s) within acceptable operating limits.
AA.VII.D.S6	Maintain airspeed ±10 knots, altitude ±100 feet, headings ±10°, as specified by the evaluator and within the airplane's capability.
AA.VII.D.S7	Consider a powerplant restart and, if appropriate, demonstrate the powerplant restart procedures in accordance with the manufacturer or operator specified procedures and checklists.
AA.VII.D.S8	Select the nearest suitable airport or landing area.
AA.VII.D.S9	Communicate with air traffic control (ATC) and the evaluator, as appropriate for the situation.

Task E. Approach and Landing with a Powerplant Failure (Simulated) (AMEL, AMES)

References: FAA-H-8083-2, FAA-H-8083-3, FAA-H-8083-25; POH/AFM; SAFO 19001

Objective: To determine the applicant exhibits satisfactory knowledge, risk management, and skills associated with approach and landing with a powerplant failure in a multiengine airplane.

Note: See Appendix 2: Safety of Flight and Appendix 3: Aircraft, Equipment, and Operational Requirements & Limitations for information related to this Task.

Knowledge:	The applicant demonstrates understanding of:
AA.VII.E.K1	Flight characteristics and controllability associated with maneuvering to a landing with inoperative powerplant(s).
AA.VII.E.K2	Go-around/rejected landing procedures with a powerplant failure.
AA.VII.E.K3	How to determine a suitable airport.

Risk Management:	The applicant is able to identify, assess, and mitigate risk associated with:
AA.VII.E.R1	Planning for a powerplant failure inflight or during an approach.
AA.VII.E.R2	Collision hazards.
AA.VII.E.R3	Configuring the airplane.
AA.VII.E.R4	Low altitude maneuvering, including stall, spin, or controlled flight into terrain (CFIT).
AA.VII.E.R5	Distractions, task prioritization, loss of situational awareness, or disorientation.
AA.VII.E.R6	Performing a go-around/rejected landing with a powerplant failure.

Skills:	The applicant exhibits the skill to:
AA.VII.E.S1	Recognize and correctly identify powerplant(s) failure, complete memory items (if applicable), and maintain positive airplane control.
AA.VII.E.S2	Coordinate with crew, if applicable, and complete the appropriate emergency procedures and checklist(s) for simulated propeller feathering or simulated powerplant shutdown.
AA.VII.E.S3	Use flight controls and configure the aircraft as required to maintain best performance or as recommended by the manufacturer.
AA.VII.E.S4	Maintain the operating powerplant(s) within acceptable operating limits.
AA.VII.E.S5	Communicate with air traffic control (ATC) and the evaluator, as appropriate for the situation.
AA.VII.E.S6	Prior to beginning the final approach segment, maintain the desired altitude ±100 feet, the desired airspeed ±10 knots, the desired heading ±5°, and accurately track courses, radials, and bearings.
AA.VII.E.S7	Establish the recommended approach and landing configuration and airspeed, ±5 knots, and adjust pitch attitude and power as required to maintain a stabilized approach.
AA.VII.E.S8	Maintain directional control and appropriate crosswind correction throughout the approach and landing.
AA.VII.E.S9	Make smooth, timely, and correct control application before, during, and after touchdown.
AA.VII.E.S10	Touch down at the appropriate speed and pitch attitude at the runway aiming point markings -250/+500 feet, or where there are no runway markings 750 to 1,500 feet from the approach threshold of the runway (AMEL).
AA.VII.E.S11	During round out and touchdown contact the water at the proper pitch attitude within 200 feet beyond a specified point. In addition, for AMES, the touchdown is within the first one-third of the water landing area.

AA.VII.E.S12	Maintain positive aircraft control throughout the landing using drag and braking devices, as appropriate, to come to a stop.
AA.VII.E.S13	Coordinate with crew, if applicable, and complete after landing checklists.

Task F. Precision Approach (Manually Flown) with a Powerplant Failure (Simulated) (AMEL, AMES)

References: FAA-H-8083-2, FAA-H-8083-3, FAA-H-8083-15, FAA-H-8083-16, FAA-H-8083-25; POH/AFM; Terminal Procedures Publications

Objective: To determine the applicant exhibits satisfactory knowledge, risk management, and skills associated with precision approach (manually flown) with a powerplant failure in a multiengine airplane.

Note: See Appendix 2: Safety of Flight and Appendix 3: Aircraft, Equipment, and Operational Requirements & Limitations for information related to this Task.

Knowledge:	The applicant demonstrates understanding of:
AA.VII.F.K1	Flight characteristics and controllability associated with maneuvering to a landing with inoperative powerplant(s).
AA.VII.F.K2	Missed approach considerations with a powerplant failure.
AA.VII.F.K3	How to determine a suitable airport.

Risk Management:	The applicant is able to identify, assess, and mitigate risk associated with:
AA.VII.F.R1	Planning for a powerplant failure inflight or during an approach.
AA.VII.F.R2	Collision hazards.
AA.VII.F.R3	Configuring the airplane.
AA.VII.F.R4	Low altitude maneuvering, including stall, spin, or controlled flight into terrain (CFIT).
AA.VII.F.R5	Distractions, task prioritization, loss of situational awareness, or disorientation.
AA.VII.F.R6	Landing with a powerplant failure.
AA.VII.F.R7	Missed approach with a powerplant failure.
AA.VII.F.R8	Maneuvering in instrument meteorological conditions (IMC) with a powerplant failure.

Skills:	The applicant exhibits the skill to:
AA.VII.F.S1	Recognize and correctly identify powerplant(s) failure, complete memory items (if applicable), and maintain positive airplane control.
AA.VII.F.S2	Coordinate with crew, if applicable, and complete the appropriate emergency procedures and checklist(s) for simulated propeller feathering or simulated powerplant shutdown.
AA.VII.F.S3	Use flight controls and configure the aircraft as required to maintain best performance or as recommended by the manufacturer.
AA.VII.F.S4	Maintain the operating powerplant(s) within acceptable operating limits.
AA.VII.F.S5	Make radio calls as appropriate.
AA.VII.F.S6	Proceed toward the nearest suitable airport.
AA.VII.F.S7	Coordinate with crew, if applicable, and complete the approach and landing checklists.

AA.VII.F.S8	Establish the appropriate airplane configuration and airspeed considering meteorological and operating conditions.
AA.VII.F.S9	Prior to beginning the final approach segment, maintain the desired altitude ±100 feet, the desired airspeed ±10 knots, the desired heading ±5°, and accurately track courses, radials, and bearings.
AA.VII.F.S10	Apply adjustments to the published decision altitude (DA)/decision height (DH) and visibility criteria for the aircraft approach category, as appropriate, for factors that include Notices to Air Missions (NOTAMs), inoperative aircraft or navigation equipment, inoperative visual aids associated with the landing environment, etc.
AA.VII.F.S11	Establish a predetermined rate of descent at the point where vertical guidance begins, which approximates that required for the aircraft to follow the vertical guidance.
AA.VII.F.S12	Fly and maintain a stabilized approach, adjusting pitch and power as required, allowing no more than ¼-scale deflection of either the vertical or lateral guidance indications.
AA.VII.F.S13	Maintain a stabilized final approach from the final approach fix (FAF) to the DA/DH allowing no more than ¼-scale deflection of either the vertical or lateral guidance indications and maintain the desired airspeed ±5 knots.
AA.VII.F.S14	Maintain directional control and appropriate crosswind correction throughout the approach and landing or missed approach.
AA.VII.F.S15	Upon reaching the DA/DH, immediately initiate the missed approach procedures if the required visual references for the runway are not distinctly visible and identifiable (or if in a seaplane); or transition to a normal landing approach only when the aircraft is in a position from which a descent to a landing on the runway can be made at a normal rate of descent using normal maneuvering.
AA.VII.F.S16	Make smooth, timely, and correct control application before, during, and after touchdown or during the missed approach.

Task G. Landing from a No Flap or a Nonstandard Flap Approach

References: *FAA-H-8083-2, FAA-H-8083-3, FAA-H-8083-25; FSB Report (type specific); POH/AFM; SAFO 19001*

Objective: To determine the applicant exhibits satisfactory knowledge, risk management, and skills associated with no flap or a nonstandard flap approach and landing.

Note: *See Appendix 3: Aircraft, Equipment, and Operational Requirements & Limitations for information related to this Task.*

Knowledge:	The applicant demonstrates understanding of:
AA.VII.G.K1	Airplane flight characteristics when flaps, leading edge devices, and other similar devices malfunction or become inoperative.
AA.VII.G.K2	Other airplane system limitations when landing at a high speed.
AA.VII.G.K3	How to determine required landing distance and a suitable runway for landing.

Risk Management:	The applicant is able to identify, assess, and mitigate risk associated with:
AA.VII.G.R1	Hazards associated with a no flap or nonstandard flap approach and landing, including an asymmetrical flap situation.
AA.VII.G.R2	Selection of a runway based on aircraft limitations, available distance, surface conditions, and wind.

AA.VII.G.R3	Wake turbulence.
AA.VII.G.R4	Go-around/rejected landing.
AA.VII.G.R5	Collision hazards.
AA.VII.G.R6	Low altitude maneuvering, including stall, spin, or controlled flight into terrain (CFIT).
AA.VII.G.R7	Distractions, task prioritization, loss of situational awareness, or disorientation.

Skills:	The applicant exhibits the skill to:
AA.VII.G.S1	Identify the malfunction.
AA.VII.G.S2	Coordinate with crew, if applicable, and complete applicable checklist(s) for the malfunction, approach, and landing.
AA.VII.G.S3	Communicate with ATC as needed and select an airport/runway with sufficient length for landing.
AA.VII.G.S4	Calculate the correct airspeeds/V-speeds for approach and landing.
AA.VII.G.S5	Establish the recommended approach and landing configuration, airspeed, and trim, and adjust pitch attitude and power as required to maintain a stabilized approach.
AA.VII.G.S6	Select a suitable touchdown point considering wind, landing surface, and obstructions.
AA.VII.G.S7	Make smooth, timely, and correct control application before, during, and after touchdown.
AA.VII.G.S8	Touch down at an acceptable point on the runway that is agreed upon between the applicant and the evaluator. Touch down at the appropriate speed and pitch attitude at the agreed upon point -250/+500 feet. (ASEL, AMEL).
AA.VII.G.S9	Touch down at an acceptable point on the landing surface. During round out and touchdown contact the water at the proper pitch attitude within 200 feet beyond a specified point (ASES, AMES). In addition, for AMES, the touchdown is within the first one-third of the water landing area.
AA.VII.G.S10	Maintain positive aircraft control throughout the landing using drag and braking devices, as appropriate, to come to a stop.

Area of Operation VIII. Postflight Procedures

Task A. After Landing, Parking, and Securing (ASEL, AMEL)

References: AIM; FAA-H-8083-2, FAA-H-8083-3, FAA-H-8083-25; POH/AFM

Objective: To determine the applicant exhibits satisfactory knowledge, risk management, and skills associated with after landing, parking, and securing procedures.

Knowledge:	The applicant demonstrates understanding of:
AA.VIII.A.K1	Parking, shutdown, securing, and postflight inspection.
AA.VIII.A.K2	Documenting in-flight/postflight discrepancies.

Risk Management:	The applicant is able to identify, assess, and mitigate risk associated with:
AA.VIII.A.R1	Activities and distractions.
AA.VIII.A.R2	[Archived]
AA.VIII.A.R3	Propeller, turbofan inlet, and exhaust safety.
AA.VIII.A.R4	Airport specific security procedures.
AA.VIII.A.R5	Disembarking passengers safely on the ramp and monitoring passenger movement while on the ramp.

Skills:	The applicant exhibits the skill to:
AA.VIII.A.S1	Use runway incursion avoidance procedures, if applicable.
AA.VIII.A.S2	Comply with air traffic control (ATC) or evaluator instructions and make radio calls as appropriate.
AA.VIII.A.S3	Coordinate with crew, if applicable, and complete the appropriate checklist(s) after clearing the runway.
AA.VIII.A.S4	Park at the gate or in an appropriate area, considering the safety of nearby persons and property.
AA.VIII.A.S5	Conduct a postflight inspection and document discrepancies and servicing requirements, if any.
AA.VIII.A.S6	Secure the airplane.

Task B. Seaplane Post-Landing Procedures (ASES, AMES)

References: AIM; FAA-H-8083-2, FAA-H-8083-3, FAA-H-8083-23, FAA-H-8083-25; POH/AFM

Objective: To determine the applicant exhibits satisfactory knowledge, risk management, and skills associated with anchoring, docking, mooring, and ramping/beaching.

Knowledge:	The applicant demonstrates understanding of:
AA.VIII.B.K1	Mooring.
AA.VIII.B.K2	Docking.
AA.VIII.B.K3	Anchoring.
AA.VIII.B.K4	Beaching/ramping.

Risk
Management: The applicant is able to identify, assess, and mitigate risk associated with:

AA.VIII.B.R1   Activities and distractions.

AA.VIII.B.R2   [Archived]

AA.VIII.B.R3   Propeller, turbofan inlet, and exhaust safety.

AA.VIII.B.R4   Airport/seaplane base security procedures.

AA.VIII.B.R5   Disembarking passengers safely on the ramp and monitoring passenger movement while on the ramp.

Skills: The applicant exhibits the skill to:

AA.VIII.B.S1   Comply with air traffic control (ATC) or evaluator instructions and make radio calls as appropriate.

AA.VIII.B.S2   If anchoring, select a suitable area considering seaplane movement, water depth, tide, wind, and weather changes. Use an adequate number of anchors and lines of sufficient strength and length to ensure the seaplane's security.

AA.VIII.B.S3   If not anchoring, approach the dock/mooring buoy or beach/ramp in the proper direction and at a safe speed, considering water depth, tide, current, and wind.

AA.VIII.B.S4   Coordinate with crew, if applicable, and complete the appropriate checklist(s).

AA.VIII.B.S5   If anchoring/mooring/beaching, secure the seaplane considering the effects of wind, waves, and changes in water level; if ramping, comply with appropriate ground movement procedures.

AA.VIII.B.S6   Conduct a postflight inspection and document discrepancies and servicing requirements, if any.

Appendix 1: Practical Test Roles, Responsibilities, and Outcomes

Eligibility Requirements for an Airline Transport Pilot Certificate

The prerequisite requirements and general eligibility for a practical test and the specific requirements for the issuance of an ATP Certificate in the airplane category can be found in 14 CFR part 61, sections 61.39(a) and 61.153.

In accordance with 14 CFR part 61, section 61.39, the applicant must pass the airman knowledge test before taking the practical test, if applicable to the certificate or rating sought.

Additional regulations in 14 CFR part 61 outline requirements for an ATP Certificate or the addition of an aircraft type rating. Some key sections include:

- 14 CFR part 61, section 61.63 for endorsement and training record requirements for an applicant seeking an airplane type rating to be added to an airman certificate (other than an ATP Certificate).
- 14 CFR part 61, section 61.155 for knowledge areas for ATP applicants.
- 14 CFR part 61, section 61.156 for training for applicants seeking a multiengine ATP Certificate.
- 14 CFR part 61, section 61.157 for the endorsement and training record requirements for an applicant seeking an airplane type rating to be added to an ATP certificate or for an airplane type rating to be concurrently completed with the original issuance of an ATP certificate.
- 14 CFR part 61, section 61.159 for aeronautical experience needed for an ATP Certificate in the airplane category;
- 14 CFR part 61, section 61.160 for the eligibility requirements for a multiengine ATP certificate with restricted privileges with reduced aeronautical experience. It also specifies the limitations that must be placed on the ATP certificate if the applicant uses this section to qualify for the certificate.
- 14 CFR part 61, section 61.165 for the addition of an airplane category or class rating to an ATP Certificate.

Applicants must pass the appropriate knowledge test listed in the table below as a prerequisite for the ATP practical test in the airplane category.

Test Code	Test Name	Number of Questions	Age	Allotted Time	Passing Score
ATS	Airline Transport Pilot Single-Engine Airplane	90	21	3.0	70
ATM	Airline Transport Pilot Multiengine Airplane	125	18	4.0	70

Use of the ACS During a Practical Test

The practical test is conducted in accordance with the ACS and FAA regulations that are current as of the date of the test.

The Areas of Operation in this ACS align with the Areas of Operation found in 14 CFR part 61, section 61.157(e). Each Area of Operation includes Tasks appropriate to that Area of Operation. Each Task contains an Objective stating what the applicant must know, consider, and/or do. The ACS then lists the aeronautical knowledge, risk management, and skill elements relevant to the specific Task, along with the conditions and standards for acceptable performance. The ACS uses Notes to emphasize special considerations.

During the ground and flight portion of the practical test, the FAA expects evaluators to assess the applicant's mastery of the topic in accordance with the level of learning most appropriate for the specified Task. The oral questioning will continue throughout the entire practical test. For some topics, the evaluator will ask the applicant to describe or explain. For other items, the evaluator will assess the applicant's understanding by providing a scenario that requires the applicant to appropriately apply and/or correlate knowledge, experience, and information to the circumstances of the given scenario. The flight portion of the practical test requires the applicant to demonstrate knowledge, risk management, flight proficiency, and operational skill in accordance with the ACS.

The elements within each Task in this ACS are coded according to a scheme that includes four components. For example, AA.I.A.K2:

AA = Applicable ACS

I = Area of Operation

A = Task

K2 = Task element (in this example, Knowledge 2)

There is no requirement for an evaluator to test every knowledge and risk management element in a Task; rather the evaluator has discretion to sample as needed to ensure the applicant's mastery of that Task. The required minimum elements to be tested from each applicable Task include:

- any elements in which the applicant was shown to be deficient on the knowledge test, as applicable;
- at least one knowledge element;
- at least one risk management element; and
- all skill elements unless otherwise noted.

The Airman Knowledge Test Report (AKTR) lists ACS codes that correlate to a specific Task element for a given Area of Operation for any incorrect responses on the knowledge test.

Knowledge and risk management elements are primarily evaluated during the knowledge testing phase of the airman certification process. The evaluator administering the practical test has the discretion to combine Tasks/elements as appropriate to testing scenarios.

Unless otherwise noted in the Task, the evaluator must test each item in the skills section by observing the applicant perform each one. As safety of flight conditions permit, the evaluator should use questions during flight to test knowledge and risk management elements not evident in the demonstrated skills. To the greatest extent practicable, evaluators should test the applicant's ability to apply and correlate information and use rote questions only when they are appropriate for the material being tested.

If the Task includes a knowledge or risk element with sub-elements, the evaluator may choose the primary element and select at least one sub-element to satisfy the requirement. Selection of the sub-element satisfies the requirement for one element unless otherwise noted.

For example, an evaluator who chooses AA.I.B.K3 may select a sub-element such as AA.I.B.K3a to satisfy the requirement to select one knowledge element

The References for each Task indicate the source material for Task elements. For example, in the Task element "Acceptable weather products and resources required for preflight planning, current and forecast weather for departure, en route, and arrival phases of flight such as:" (AA.I.C.K2), the applicant should be prepared for questions on any weather product presented in the references for that Task.

The abbreviation(s) within parentheses immediately following a Task refer to the category and/or class aircraft appropriate to that Task. Those tasks that have the ATP abbreviation in parenthesis within the Task title (e.g., Weather Information (ATP)) are required for an ATP practical test, but are not required for a type rating only practical test. The meaning of each abbreviation is as follows.

- ATP—ATP Certificate only
- ASEL—Airplane – Single-Engine Land
- ASES—Airplane – Single-Engine Sea
- AMEL—Airplane – Multiengine Land
- AMES—Airplane – Multiengine Sea

Note: *When administering a test, the Tasks appropriate to the class airplane (ASEL, ASES, AMEL, or AMES) used for the test must be included in the plan of action.*

The FAA encourages applicants and instructors to use the ACS when preparing for the airman knowledge tests and practical tests. Evaluators must conduct the practical test in accordance with the current ACS and FAA regulations pursuant to 14 CFR part 61, section 61.43. If an applicant is entitled to credit for Areas of Operation previously passed as indicated on a Notice of Disapproval of Application or Letter of Discontinuance, evaluators shall use the ACS currently in effect on the date of the test.

The ground portion of the practical test allows the evaluator to determine whether the applicant is sufficiently prepared to advance to the flight portion of the practical test. The applicant must pass the ground portion of the practical test before beginning the flight portion. The oral questioning will continue throughout the entire practical test.

Instructor Responsibilities

The instructor trains and qualifies the applicant to meet the established standards for knowledge, risk management, and skill elements in all Tasks appropriate to the certificate and rating sought. The instructor should use this ACS and its references when preparing the applicant to take the practical test and when retraining the applicant to proficiency in any subject(s) missed on the knowledge test.

Evaluator Responsibilities

An evaluator includes the following:

- Aviation Safety Inspector (ASI);
- Pilot examiner (other than administrative pilot examiners);
- Training center evaluator (TCE);
- Chief instructor, assistant chief instructor, or check instructor of pilot school holding examining authority; or
- Instrument Flight Instructor (CFII) conducting an instrument proficiency check (IPC).

The evaluator who conducts the practical test verifies the applicant has met the aeronautical experience requirements specified for a certificate or rating before administering the test. During the practical test, the evaluator determines whether the applicant meets the established standards of aeronautical knowledge, risk management, and skills for the Tasks in the appropriate ACS.

The evaluator must develop a plan of action (POA) that includes all required Areas of Operation and Tasks and administer each practical test in English. The POA must include scenario(s) that evaluate as many of the required Areas of Operation and Tasks as possible. As a scenario unfolds during the test, the evaluator will introduce problems and simulate emergencies that test the applicant's ability. The evaluator has the discretion to modify the POA to accommodate unexpected situations as they arise or suspend and later resume a scenario to assess certain Tasks.

Prior to and throughout the evaluation, the evaluator ensures the applicant meets the FAA Aviation English Language Standard (AELS). An applicant must be able to communicate in English in a discernible and understandable manner with air traffic control (ATC), pilots, and others involved in preparing an aircraft for flight and operating an aircraft in flight. This communication may or may not involve radio communications. An applicant for an FAA certificate or rating issued in accordance with 14 CFR parts 61, 63, 65, or 107 who cannot hear or speak due to a medical deficiency may be eligible for an FAA certificate with specific operational limitations.

If the applicant's ability to meet the FAA AELS comes into question before starting the practical test, the evaluator will not begin the practical test. An evaluator other than an ASI will check the box, "Referred to FSO for Aviation English Language Standard Determination," located on the bottom of page 2 of the applicant's FAA Form 8710-1, Airman Certificate and/or Rating Application, or FAA Form 8710-11, Airman Certificate and/or Rating Application - Sport Pilot, as applicable. The evaluator will refer the applicant to the appropriate Flight Standards Office (FSO).

If the applicant's ability to meet the FAA AELS comes into question after the practical test begins, an evaluator who other than an ASI will discontinue the practical test and check the box, "Referred to FSO for Aviation English Language Standard Determination," on the application. The evaluator will also issue FAA Form 8060-5, Notice of Disapproval of Application, with the comment "Does Not Demonstrate FAA AELS" in addition to any unsatisfactory Task(s). The evaluator will refer the applicant to the appropriate FSO. ASIs conducting the practical test may assess an applicant's English language proficiency in accordance with FAA Order 8900.1.

In either case, the evaluator must complete and submit the application file through normal application procedures and evaluators other than an ASI notify the appropriate FSO of the referral.

If the ability of an FAA certificated airman comes into question prior to or during a required regulatory check (e.g., proficiency check) the evaluator other than an ASI will not continue the check or provide an endorsement indicating completion. The evaluator will refer the airman to the jurisdictional FAA field office for further determination of ability to meet the FAA AELS.

For additional information, reference AC 60-28, FAA English Language Standard for an FAA Certificate issued under 14 CFR parts 61, 63, 65, and 107, as amended.

Possible Outcomes of the Test

A practical test has three possible outcomes: (1) Temporary Airman Certificate (satisfactory), (2) Notice of Disapproval of Application (unsatisfactory), or (3) Letter of Discontinuance.

If the evaluator determines that a Task is incomplete, or the outcome is uncertain, the evaluator must require the applicant to repeat that Task, or portions of that Task. This provision does not mean that instruction, practice, or the repetition of an unsatisfactory Task is permitted during the practical test.

Satisfactory Performance

Refer to 14 CFR part 61, section 61.43, for satisfactory performance requirements.

Satisfactory performance will result in the issuance of a temporary certificate.

Depending upon the pilot flight crew complement required for the test, the pilot is expected to demonstrate competence in crew resource management in an operation or airplane certificated for more than one required pilot crewmember, or single-pilot competence in an operation or airplane that is certificated for single-pilot operations.

If a successful check is conducted under an operator's approved training and checking program, it is considered to have met the flight proficiency requirements of 14 CFR part 61, section 61.157(f) for the issuance of an ATP certificate and an appropriate rating. An evaluator that conducts ATP certificate evaluations in accordance with an approved 91K, part 121, or part 135 training and checking program is not required to use this document.

Unsatisfactory Performance

If, in the judgment of the evaluator, the applicant does not meet the standards for any Task, the applicant fails the Task and associated Area of Operation and the evaluator issues a Notice of Disapproval of Application. The evaluator lists the Area(s) of Operation in which the applicant did not meet the standard, any Area(s) of Operation not tested, and the number of practical test failures. The evaluator should also list the Tasks failed or Tasks not tested within any unsatisfactory or partially completed Area(s) of Operation. 14 CFR part 61, section 61.43(c)–(f) provides additional unsatisfactory performance requirements and parameters.

Typical areas of unsatisfactory performance and grounds for disqualification include:

- Any action or lack of action by the applicant that requires corrective intervention by the evaluator to maintain safe flight.
- Failure to use proper and effective visual scanning techniques to clear the area before and while performing maneuvers.
- Consistently exceeding tolerances stated in the skill elements of the Task.
- Failure to take prompt corrective action when tolerances are exceeded.
- Failure to exercise risk management.

The evaluator or the applicant may end the test if the applicant fails a Task. The evaluator may continue the test only with the consent of the applicant. The applicant receives credit only for those Areas of Operation and the associated Tasks performed satisfactorily.

Letter of Discontinuance

Refer to 14 CFR part 61, section 61.43(e)(2) for conditions to issue a letter of discontinuance.

If discontinuing a practical test for reasons other than unsatisfactory performance (e.g., equipment failure, weather, illness), the evaluator must return all test paperwork to the applicant. The evaluator must prepare, sign, and issue a Letter of Discontinuance that lists those Areas of Operation the applicant successfully completed and the time period remaining to complete the test to receive credit for previously completed Areas of Operation. The evaluator should advise the applicant to present the Letter of Discontinuance to the evaluator when the practical test resumes in order to receive credit for the items successfully completed. The Letter of Discontinuance becomes part of the applicant's certification file.

Time Limit and Credit after a Discontinued Practical Test

Refer to 14 CFR part 61, sections 61.39(f) and 61.43(f) after issuance of a Letter of Discontinuance or Notice of Disapproval of Application.

ATP Certificate Task Table

Each column title in the table below identifies the airplane category and class rating sought on the ATP certificate. This table applies to initial ATP applicants and applicants seeking additional ratings. The evaluator must evaluate the applicant in the Areas of Operation and Tasks listed in the table below. The evaluator has the discretion to evaluate the applicant's competence in the remaining Areas of Operation and Tasks.

Area of Operation	Airplane Single-Engine – Land[a]	Airplane Single-Engine – Sea[a]	Airplane Multiengine – Land[b]	Airplane Multiengine – Sea[b,c]
I	A,B,C,F,G	A,B,C,F,G,H	A,B,C,D,E,F,G	All
II	A,B,C,E	A,B,D,E	A,B,C,E	A,B,D,E
III	A,B,I,J	All	A,B,I,J	All
IV	All	All	All	All
V	All	All	All	All
VI	All	All	All	All
VII	A,B,C,G	A,B,C,G	A,B,D,E,F,G	A,B,D,E,F,G
VIII	A	B	A	B

a. An applicant with qualifications other than a commercial pilot certificate in the airplane category and a single- engine class rating who applies for an ATP certificate in the airplane category with a single-engine class rating (ASEL or ASES) must also demonstrate the following Tasks based upon the applicant's qualifications at the time of the ATP practical test:

- If the applicant has not completed a commercial practical test in a single-engine airplane, evaluators must test the Power-Off 180° Accuracy Approach and Landing Task in accordance with the Commercial Pilot for Airplane Category ACS (FAA-S-ACS-7, as amended), Area of Operation IV, Task M. (Ref. 14 CFR part 61, sections 61.153 and 61.165(b) and (e)).

- If the applicant does not hold an airman certificate with an airplane single-engine class rating, evaluators must test both the Forward Slip to the Landing Task in accordance with the Private Pilot for Airplane Category ACS (FAA-S-ACS-6 as amended), Area of Operation IV, Task M and a Power-Off 180° Accuracy Approach and Landing Task, Commercial Pilot for Airplane Category ACS (FAA-S-ACS-7 as amended), Area of Operation IV, Task M. (Ref. 14 CFR part 61, sections 61.153 and 61.165(b) and (e)).

b. If an applicant does not hold an airplane multiengine class rating on his or her current pilot certificate, or current airplane multiengine rating or multiengine type rating on a foreign license, evaluators must test the Maneuvering with One Engine Inoperative Task and the V_{MC} Demonstration Task in accordance with the Commercial Pilot for Airplane Category ACS (FAA-S-ACS-7, as amended), Area of Operation X, Tasks A and B. Note that holding an second-in-command (SIC) pilot type rating does not remove this testing requirement.

c. When adding the Airplane Multiengine Sea Rating to an existing ATP Airplane Multiengine Land Certificate, the applicant may supply a seaplane without propeller feathering capability and perform simulated propeller feathering during the practical test.

Addition of a Type Rating to an Existing Pilot Certificate and Proficiency Check Requirements

In accordance with 14 CFR part 61, sections 61.63 and 61.157, the table below identifies the Tasks required for the category and class of type rating sought. No Task credit exists for an SIC pilot type rating issued in accordance with 14 CFR part 61, section 61.55.

Note: *Available type ratings can be located in FAA Order 8900.1, Volume 5, Chapter 2, Section 19.*

In accordance with 14 CFR part 61, section 61.58(d)(1), the table below also identifies the Tasks required for a proficiency check.

Area of Operation	Airplane Single-Engine – Land	Airplane Multiengine – Land	Airplane Single-Engine – Sea	Airplane Multiengine – Sea
I	A,B	A,B	A,B,H	A,B,H
II	A,B,C,E	A,B,C,E	A,B,D,E	A,B,D,E
III	A,B,I,J	A,B,I,J	All	All
IV	All	All	All	All
V	All	All	All	All
VI	All	All	All	All
VII	A,B,C,G	A,B,D,E,F,G	A,B,C,G	A,B,D,E,F,G
VIII	A	A	B	B

Addition of a VFR Only Type Rating to an Existing Pilot Certificate

Refer to 14 CFR section 61.63(e) or section 61.157(g), as applicable. An applicant may add a type rating to a pilot certificate for an airplane type not capable of instrument flight without performing Tasks by reference to instruments during the practical test. This results in a "VFR only" limitation for the type rating on the pilot certificate. The following table identifies the Tasks required for the category and class of type rating sought. Each column title identifies the class of the type rating sought on an existing pilot certificate.

Area of Operation	Airplane Multiengine – Land	Airplane Single-Engine – Land	Airplane Multiengine – Sea	Airplane Single-Engine – Sea
I	A,B	A,B	A,B,H	A,B,H
II	A,B,C,E	A,B,C,E	A,B,D,E	A,B,D,E
III	A,B,I,J	A,B,I,J	All	All
IV	All	All	All	All
V	All	All	All	All
VI	None	None	None	None
VII	A,B,D,E,G	A,B,C,G	A,B,D,E,G	A,B,C,G
VIII	A	A	B	B

Note: *The Tasks listed above that are normally required to be performed by reference to instruments would be conducted using visual references for the purposes of a VFR only type rating.*

Removal of the "Second in Command Required" Limitation from a Type Rating

A pilot, who holds an airplane type rating with a "Second-In-Command Required" Limitation, may test to remove the limitation and receive an unrestricted type rating. During the practical test, the pilot must demonstrate single-pilot competency in the Areas of Operation and Tasks listed below.

Area of Operation	Airplane Multiengine – Land Tasks	Airplane Multiengine – Sea Tasks
I	None	None
II	A,B,C,E	A,B,D,E
III	A,B,I,J	All
IV	B,C	B,C
V	None	None
VI	All	All
VII	A,B,D,E,F,G	A,B,D,E,F,G
VIII	A	B

Removal of Circle-to-Land Limitation on an ATP Certificate or Type Rating

A pilot may receive a circle-to-land limitation through an approved air carrier training and checking program restricting a circling approach to visual meteorological conditions (V_{MC}) only. Depending on pilot qualifications the limitation may apply to the ATP pilot certificate, associated type rating(s), or both. In order to remove a circling limitation, the applicant must be tested by a qualified evaluator on Tasks G and H of Area of Operation VI within this ACS.

This restriction, "ATP CIRC APCH V_{MC} ONLY," may be removed from the ATP certificate upon completion of an evaluation of the circling maneuver tasks in an airplane representative of the class held on the applicant's ATP certificate. The airplane used does not have to be type-specific, but must reflect a class of airplane for which the pilot has ATP privileges. The limitation removal may involve training depending on the airplane used.

For removal of the circle-to-land limitation pertaining to a specific airplane type rating, the airplane used for the test must represent the airplane type to which the restriction applies. Removal of a circle-to-land limitation from a type rating will also remove the limitation, "ATP CIRC APCH V_{MC} ONLY" (if applicable). However, the circle-to-land limitation will remain on any other type rating(s) the pilot holds with a limitation until the pilot has been tested in that specific aircraft type for the removal of the limitation.

> **Note:** *The requirements for the removal of the circle-to-land limitation(s) may be completed in an FSTD if conducted in accordance with an approved training program.*

Airplane Multiengine Land Limited to Center Thrust

When conducting a practical test for a pilot that has not previously demonstrated competence in a multiengine airplane with a published V_{MC}, or when removing the center thrust limitation from the AMEL rating, the evaluator must test the applicant on the following Areas of Operation and Tasks from the Airline Transport Pilot and Type Rating for Airplane Category ACS (FAA-S-ACS-11, as amended) and Commercial Pilot for Airplane Category ACS (FAA-S-ACS-7, as amended) in a multiengine airplane that has a manufacturer's published V_{MC} speed. This speed can be found on the type certificate data sheet (TCDS) or in the AFM. If the limitation will be removed under part 121, 135, or 142, it must be done in accordance with an approved curriculum or training program.

Airline Transport Pilot and Type Rating for Airplane Category ACS (FAA-S-ACS-11 as amended)

Area of Operation	Required Tasks
III	I
VII	B,D,E

Commercial Pilot –for Airplane Category ACS (FAA-S-ACS-7 as amended)

Area of Operation	Required Tasks
X	A,B

Appendix 2: Safety of Flight

General

Safety of flight must be the prime consideration at all times. The evaluator, applicant, and crew must be continually alert for other traffic. If performing aspects of a given maneuver, such as emergency procedures, would jeopardize safety, the evaluator will ask the applicant to simulate that portion of the maneuver. The evaluator will assess the applicant's use of visual scanning and collision avoidance procedures throughout the entire test.

Stall and Spin Awareness

During flight training and testing, the applicant and the instructor or evaluator must always recognize and avoid operations that could lead to an inadvertent stall or spin and inadvertent loss of control.

Use of Checklists

Throughout the practical test, the applicant is evaluated on the use of an appropriate checklist.

Assessing proper checklist use depends upon the specific Task. In all cases, the evaluator should determine whether the applicant demonstrates CRM, appropriately divides attention, and uses proper visual scanning. In some situations, reading the actual checklist may be impractical or unsafe. In such cases, the evaluator should assess the applicant's performance of published or recommended immediate action "memory" items along with their review of the appropriate checklist once conditions permit.

In a single-pilot aircraft, the applicant should demonstrate the crew resource management (CRM) principles described as single-pilot resource management (SRM). Proper use depends on the specific Task being evaluated. If the use of the checklist while accomplishing elements of an Objective would be either unsafe or impractical in a single-pilot operation, the applicant should review the checklist after accomplishing the elements.

Positive Exchange of Flight Controls

A clear understanding of who has control of the aircraft must exist. Prior to flight, the pilots involved should conduct a briefing that includes reviewing the procedures for exchanging flight controls.

The FAA recommends a positive three-step process for exchanging flight controls between pilots:

- When one pilot seeks to have the other pilot take control of the aircraft, they will say, "You have the flight controls."
- The second pilot acknowledges immediately by saying, "I have the flight controls."
- The first pilot again says, "You have the flight controls," and visually confirms the exchange.

Pilots should follow this procedure during any exchange of flight controls, including any occurrence during the practical test. The FAA also recommends that both pilots use a visual check to verify that the exchange has occurred. Doubt as to who is flying the aircraft should not occur.

Use of Distractions

Numerous studies indicate that many accidents have occurred when the pilot has been distracted during critical phases of flight. The evaluator should incorporate realistic distractions during the flight portion of the practical test to evaluate the pilot's situational awareness and ability to utilize proper control technique while dividing attention both inside and outside the flight deck.

Aeronautical Decision-Making, Risk Management, Crew Resource Management, and Single-Pilot Resource Management

Throughout the practical test, the evaluator must assess the applicant's ability to use sound aeronautical decision-making procedures in order to identify hazards and mitigate risk. The evaluator must accomplish this requirement by reference to the risk management elements of the given Task(s), and by developing scenarios that incorporate and combine Tasks appropriate to assessing the applicant's risk management in making safe aeronautical decisions. For example, the evaluator may develop a scenario that incorporates weather decisions and performance planning.

In assessing the applicant's performance, the evaluator should take note of the applicant's use of CRM and, if appropriate, SRM. CRM/SRM is the set of competencies that includes situational awareness, communication skills, teamwork, task allocation, and decision-making within a comprehensive framework of standard operating procedures (SOP). SRM specifically refers to the management of all resources onboard the aircraft, as well as outside resources available to the single pilot.

An evaluator, other than an FAA Inspector, qualified as a safety pilot, and current in the specific make and model aircraft certified for two or more crewmembers may occupy a duty position. If occupying a duty position on an aircraft that requires two or more crewmembers, the evaluator must fulfill the duties of that position. Moreover, when occupying a required duty position, the evaluator must perform CRM functions as briefed and requested by the applicant except during the accomplishment of steep turns, approach to stalls, and recovery from unusual attitudes. During these Tasks the applicant must demonstrate the ability to control the aircraft without the intervention from the pilot monitoring. However, for aircraft requiring only one pilot, the evaluator may not assist the applicant in the management of the aircraft, radio communications, tuning and identifying navigational equipment, or using navigation charts.

Multiengine Considerations

For safety reasons, when the practical test is conducted in an airplane, the applicant must perform Tasks that require powerplant shutdown or propeller feathering only under conditions and at a position and altitude where it is possible to make a safe landing on an established airport if there is difficulty in restarting the powerplant or unfeathering the propeller. The evaluator must select an entry altitude that will allow the Powerplant Failure Tasks to be completed no lower than 3,000 feet AGL or the manufacturer's recommended altitude, whichever is higher. If it is not possible to restart the powerplant or unfeather the propeller while airborne, the applicant and the evaluator should treat the situation as an emergency.

At altitudes lower than 3,000 feet AGL, powerplant failure should be simulated as recommended by the manufacturer. For propeller-driven airplanes, powerplant failure should be simulated by reducing throttle to idle and then establishing zero thrust. For additional Task considerations, see Appendix 3: Aircraft, Equipment, and Operational Requirements & Limitations, Area of Operation III, Takeoffs and Landings, Task I. Rejected Takeoff, and the powerplant failure Tasks in Area of Operation VII. Emergency Operations.

Except for a type rating practical test, for an airplane equipped with propellers (including turboprop), the applicant must feather one propeller and shut down an engine unless the manufacturer prohibits it. However, if an applicant has not previously demonstrated multiengine airplane tasks for the commercial pilot certificate, the applicant cannot use a propeller-equipped airplane where the manufacturer prohibits feathering for the initial ATP multiengine airplane certificate. If the practical test is conducted in an airplane that requires the pilot to hold a type rating, the applicant may perform a simulated powerplant failure. In all other cases, the applicant must feather and unfeather the propeller while airborne.

Practical tests conducted in an FSTD can only be accomplished as part of an approved curriculum or training program. Any limitations on powerplant failure will be noted in that program. In addition, an evaluator may reference an airplane's FSB report, which may include other safety related considerations for performing specific tasks.

Single-Engine Considerations

For safety reasons, the evaluator will not request a simulated powerplant failure in a single-engine airplane unless it is possible to safely complete a landing.

For airplanes that have an FSB Report, reference it for any other safety related considerations in performing specific tasks.

High-Performance Airplane Considerations

In some high performance airplanes, the power setting may have to be reduced below the suggested power setting in this ACS to prevent excessively high pitch attitudes greater than 30° nose up.

Appendix 3: Aircraft, Equipment, and Operational Requirements & Limitations

Aircraft Requirements & Limitations

If the aircraft has inoperative equipment and can be operated in accordance with 14 CFR part 91, section 91.213, it must be determined if any inoperative instruments or equipment are required to complete the practical test. The inoperative equipment must not interfere with practical test requirements.

Multiengine practical tests require normal engine shutdowns and restarts in the air, to include propeller feathering and unfeathering. The Airplane Flight Manual (AFM) must not prohibit these procedures, but low power settings for cooling periods prior to the actual shutdown in accordance with the AFM are acceptable and encouraged. For a type rating in an airplane not certificated with inflight unfeathering capability, a simulated powerplant failure is acceptable.

Equipment Requirements & Limitations

The aircraft must meet the requirements as outlined in 14 CFR part 61, section 61.45.

To assist in management of the aircraft during the practical test, the applicant is expected to demonstrate automation management skills by utilizing installed, available, or airborne equipment such as autopilot, avionics and systems displays, and/or a flight management system (FMS). The evaluator is expected to test the applicant's knowledge of the systems that are available or installed and operative during both the ground and flight portions of the practical test. If the applicant has trained using a portable electronic flight bag (EFB) to display charts and data and wishes to use the EFB during the practical test, the applicant is expected to demonstrate appropriate knowledge, risk management, and skill appropriate to its use.

If the practical test involves maneuvering the aircraft solely by reference to instruments, the applicant is required by 14 CFR part 61, section 61.45(d)(2) to provide an appropriate view limiting device acceptable to the Administrator. The applicant and the evaluator should establish a procedure as to when and how this device should be donned and removed and brief this procedure before the flight. This device must prevent the applicant from having visual reference outside the aircraft, but it must not restrict the evaluator's ability to see and avoid other traffic. The use of the device does not apply to specific elements within a Task when there is a requirement for visual references.

If a type rating practical test is given in an amphibious airplane, the type rating must bear the limitation "Limited to Land" or "Limited to Sea," as appropriate, unless the applicant demonstrates proficiency in both land and sea operations.

Use of Flight Simulation Training Devices (FSTD)

Applicants for a pilot certificate or rating can accomplish all or part of a practical test or proficiency check in an FSTD qualified under 14 CFR part 60, which includes full flight simulators (FFS) or flight training devices (FTD), only when conducted within an FAA-approved training program. Each operational rule part identifies additional requirements for the approval and use of FSTDs in an FAA-approved training program.

Credit for Pilot Time in an FSTD

14 CFR part 61 and part 141 specify the minimum experience requirements for each certificate or rating sought. 14 CFR part 61 and the appendices to part 141 specify the maximum amount of FFS or FTD flight training time an applicant can apply toward those experience requirements.

Use of Aviation Training Devices (ATD)

Applicants for a pilot certificate or rating cannot use an ATD to accomplish a practical test, a 14 CFR part 61, section 61.58 proficiency check, or the flight portion of a 14 CFR part 61, section 61.57 flight review. An ATD is defined in 14 CFR part 61, section 61.1.

The FAA's General Aviation and Commercial Division evaluates and approves ATDs as permitted under 14 CFR part 61, section 61.4(c) and FAA Order 8900.1. Each ATD is then issued an FAA letter of authorization (LOA) that is valid for 60 calendar months. The LOA for each ATD lists the pilot time credit allowances and associated limitations.

The Pilot Training and Certification Group public website provides a list of the FAA-approved ATDs and the associated manufacturer.

Credit for Pilot Time in an ATD

14 CFR part 61 and part 141 specify the minimum experience requirements for each certificate or rating sought. 14 CFR part 61 and the appendices to part 141 specify the maximum amount of ATD flight training time an applicant can apply toward those experience requirements. The LOA for each FAA-approved ATD lists the pilot time credit allowances and the associated limitations.

Evaluators must request an applicant to provide a copy of the manufacturer's LOA when using ATD flight training time credit to meet the minimum experience requirements for an airman pilot certificate, rating, or privilege.

Operational Requirements, Limitations, & Task Information

The applicant must perform the tasks in Areas of Operation IV through VII in actual or simulated instrument conditions, except for:

- Testing of elements that require visual maneuvering; or
- When the aircraft's type certificate makes the aircraft incapable of operating under instrument flight rules (IFR). See Appendix 1—Practical Test Roles, Responsibilities, and Outcomes for required Tasks to be completed for a VFR Only type rating.
- Preflight Preparation

Task A. Operation of Systems

All certificates, ratings, and type ratings include testing this Task, which focuses on systems knowledge for the ATP certificate and the type rating for the airplane brought to the test. The knowledge elements in Task A include a broad categorization of airplane systems, and each element has examples of the content that the evaluator could ask about for the airplane brought for the practical test. Although the examples are comprehensive, they are not necessarily all-inclusive. The applicant explains an airplane's systems and components as part of the oral portion of the practical test.

The evaluator may assess certain Skill elements in this Task during the oral portion of the practical test. The Skill elements test an applicant's systems knowledge based upon the aircraft provided in order to adequately evaluate the applicant's knowledge, understanding, and skill for the specific airplane systems, its components, checklists, and procedures.

Task B. Performance and Limitations

All certificates, ratings, and type ratings include testing this Task. When a practical test does not require an FAA airman knowledge test (AKT), the evaluator selects at least one Knowledge element and should tailor the questions towards the actual airplane provided for the practical test. If the applicant took and passed a required an AKT and missed any Knowledge elements for this Task, the evaluator may ask general or airplane specific questions on performance charts, performance calculations, and factors that affect airplane performance.

Evaluators may assess certain Skill elements in Task B during the oral portion of the practical test. For example, the Skill elements test an applicant's knowledge and understanding of aircraft performance and the ability to calculate weight and balance specific to the aircraft provided.

Task C. Weather Information (ATP)

The applicant may use any risk assessment tool provided it allows for risk assessment and mitigation. This Task is not required for aircraft type rating only applicants.

Task D. High Altitude Aerodynamics (ATP) (AMEL) (AMES)

The specific content in this Task is included in the training required for multiengine applicants in accordance with section 61.156 regardless of the multiengine airplane brought for the practical test. This Task is only required for applicants seeking a multiengine class rating on the ATP certificate. This Task is not required for aircraft type rating only applicants. This Task is also not required for applicants seeking an ATP certificate with a single-engine class rating (initial or add-on) or applicants adding a single-engine airplane type rating to a pilot certificate.

Task E. Air Carrier Operations (ATP) (AMEL, AMES)

The specific content in this Task is included in the training required for multiengine applicants in accordance with section 61.156 regardless of the multiengine airplane brought for the practical test. This Task is only required for applicants seeking a multiengine class rating on the ATP certificate. This Task is not required for aircraft type rating only applicants. This Task is also not required for applicants seeking an ATP certificate with a single-engine class rating (initial or add-on) or applicants adding a single-engine airplane type rating to a pilot certificate.

Task F. Human Factors (ATP)

The ability to perform a self-assessment and determine fitness for flight applies to practical tests given in an airplane or a flight simulation training device (FSTD). This Task is not required for aircraft type rating only applicants.

Task G. The Code of Federal Regulations (ATP)

The evaluator has discretion to choose a representative sampling of one or more rule parts. The single-engine airman knowledge test covers part 14 CFR part 135, while a multiengine airplane airman knowledge tests covers 14 CFR parts 117 and 121. The practical test covers the relevant subparts listed in the elements applicable to the test taken. This Task is not required for aircraft type rating only applicants.

II. Preflight Procedures

Task A. Preflight Assessment

The testing of Task A must occur prior to all other portions of the preflight procedures area of operation, and must be completed prior to the flight portion of the practical test. A part 142 training curriculum may use a pictorial aircraft preflight inspection program.

For a particular type of airplane with a Flight Engineer as a required crewmember, the evaluator may waive the actual visual inspection and use an approved pictorial means that realistically portrays the location and detail of inspection items. On airplanes requiring a flight engineer, an applicant must demonstrate satisfactory knowledge of the flight engineer functions for the safe completion of the flight if the flight engineer becomes ill or incapacitated during a flight.

Task B. Powerplant Start

For practical tests in an airplane, evaluators may assess an applicant's ability to respond to a powerplant start failure or malfunction through scenario-based oral questioning.

Task E. Before Takeoff Checks

Each applicant must give a briefing before each takeoff. If the operator or aircraft manufacturer has not specified a briefing, the briefing must cover the items appropriate for the conditions, such as: departure runway, departure procedure, power settings, speeds, abnormal or emergency procedures prior to or after reaching decision speed (i.e., V_1 or V_{MC}), emergency return intentions, and what the applicant expects other crewmembers to do during the takeoff/departure, if applicable. If the applicant provides a satisfactory briefing before the first takeoff, the evaluator may allow the applicant to brief only the changes, during the remainder of the test. For single-pilot operations, the applicant must verbalize the briefings.

III. Takeoffs and Landings

The applicant must make at least three actual landings with at least one to a full stop. The evaluator may combine Landing Tasks where appropriate to include the Landing Tasks found in the Instrument Procedures Area of Operation and the Emergency Operations Area of Operation.

Briefings

Each applicant must give a briefing before each takeoff and landing. If the operator, aircraft manufacturer, or training provider has not specified a briefing, the briefing must cover the items appropriate for the conditions, such as: departure runway, departure procedure, power settings, speeds, abnormal or emergency procedures prior to or after reaching decision speed (i.e., V_1 or V_{MC}), emergency return intentions, go-around/rejected landing procedures, initial rate of descent, and what is expected of the other crewmembers during the takeoff and landing. For single-pilot operations, the applicant must verbalize the briefings. If the first takeoff and landing briefings are satisfactory, the evaluator may allow the applicant to brief only the changes, during the remainder of the evaluation.

Task A. Normal Takeoff and Climb

A normal takeoff begins from a standing or rolling start (not from a touch-and-go) with all engines operating normally during the takeoff and initial climb phase. For a flight test conducted in an airplane, evaluators may have very little control over existing meteorological, airport, and traffic conditions. Evaluators should attempt to evaluate a takeoff on a runway not favorably aligned with the prevailing wind, but may have no other option than to rely on the crosswind component that exists on the active runway.

For takeoffs evaluated in a full flight simulator (FFS), the crosswind component entered in the instructor operating station (IOS) should be between 10 and 15 knots. However, the evaluator has discretion to use a crosswind component greater than 15 knots, but not above the crosswind component allowed by the operator's aircraft operating manual or the maximum demonstrated value given in the approved flight manual.

Task B. Normal Approach and Landing

The evaluator should test at least one of the required landings while the applicant manually controls the airplane in a crosswind. When the flight test occurs in an airplane, evaluators may have very little control over existing meteorological, airport, and traffic conditions. Evaluators should make a reasonable attempt to evaluate a landing on a runway not favorably aligned with the prevailing wind, but may have no other option than to rely on the crosswind component that exists on the active runway.

For landings evaluated in a full flight simulator (FFS), the crosswind component entered in the instructor operating station (IOS) should be between 10 and 15 knots. However, the evaluator has discretion to use a crosswind component greater than 15 knots, but not above the crosswind component allowed by the operator's aircraft operating manual or the maximum demonstrated value given in the approved AFM.

Task G. Confined-Area Takeoff and Maximum Performance Climb (ASES, AMES)

This Task simulates a takeoff from an area that would require a takeoff and spiral climb; or a straight-ahead takeoff and climb from a narrow waterway with obstructions at either end. The evaluator must assess both takeoff situations for this Task.

In multiengine seaplanes or amphibians with V_X values within 5 knots of V_{MC}, the applicant and evaluator may brief using V_Y or the manufacturer's recommendation if more appropriate for this demonstration.

Task H. Confined-Area Approach and Landing (ASES, AMES)

This Task simulates an approach and landing to a small pond, which would require a spiral approach, wings level landing, and step turn upon landing; or a straight-ahead approach and landing to a narrow waterway with obstructions at either end. The evaluator must evaluate both landing situations for this Task.

Task I. Rejected Takeoff

If completed in a multiengine airplane, the powerplant failure must be simulated before reaching 50 percent of V_{MC}.

Task J. Go-Around/Rejected Landing

The instrument conditions need not be simulated below 100 feet above the runway. This maneuver should be initiated approximately 50 feet above the runway or landing area and approximately over the runway threshold.

For those applicants seeking a VFR-only type rating and where this maneuver is accomplished with a simulated engine failure, it should not be initiated at speeds or altitudes below that recommended in the AFM/POH.

Completion of this Task may count for one of the three required actual landings. Wheel contact with the runway is not required.

IV. Inflight Maneuvers

Task A. Steep Turns

The applicant must demonstrate his or her ability to control the airplane manually without any intervention from the pilot monitoring, if applicable, or the evaluator. Use of available aircraft instrumentation is acceptable.

This Task is to be conducted by reference to instruments. If IFR, the pilots should be situationally aware of location and any potential traffic.

For a VFR-only type rating, this Task will be performed in visual conditions and the pilot should clear the area of traffic prior to beginning the maneuver; AA.IV.A.S3 would not be required to be by reference to instruments.

Task C. Specific Flight Characteristics

The evaluator only tests this Task if the airplane has specific flight characteristics identified in the Flight Standardization Board Report (FSBR).

V. Stall Prevention

The applicant must demonstrate the ability to control the aircraft without the intervention from the pilot monitoring, if applicable.

When testing Tasks A, B, and C, one stall must be induced while in a turn with a bank angle of 15-30 degrees; and, one stall should be induced by commands to the autopilot, if installed. In addition, these Tasks should be accomplished by reference to flight instruments. For a VFR only type rating, however, the Tasks should be accomplished in visual conditions.

When conducted in the airplane and when necessary for operational considerations, the applicant should limit power application in accordance with the evaluator's instructions.

An impending stall means the same as an approach-to-stall or the first indication of a stall. As noted in AC 120-109 (as amended), an impending stall occurs when the angle of attack causes a stall warning. In accordance with aircraft certification standards, a stall warning must be furnished by inherent aerodynamics (e.g., buffet) or an acceptable stall warning device (e.g., stick shaker). The intent of the Task is evaluate recognition of the stall warning and execution of the proper stall recovery procedure. Other warnings, cautions, or alerts that do not meet the definition of a stall warning, such as a low airspeed warning, cannot be used as an indication of an impending stall for completion of these stall Tasks

Evaluation criteria for a recovery from an impending stall must not mandate a predetermined value for altitude loss and must not mandate maintaining altitude during recovery. Valid evaluation criteria must take into account the multitude of external (such as density altitude) and internal variables (e.g., aircraft mass, drag configuration and powerplant response time) which affect the recovery altitude.

Reference the airplane flight manual or FSBR, if available, for any aircraft-specific considerations concerning stalls.

Task A. Partial Flap Configuration Stall Prevention

When accomplished in a flight simulation training device (FSTD), the entry should be consistent with the expected operational environment for a stall on takeoff or while on approach in a partial flap configuration with no minimum entry altitude defined.

Task B. Clean Configuration Stall Prevention

When accomplished in an FSTD, the entry should be consistent with the expected operational environment for a stall in cruise flight with no minimum entry altitude defined.

Task C. Landing Configuration Stall Prevention

When accomplished in an FSTD, the entry should be consistent with the expected operational environment for a stall when fully configured for landing with no minimum entry altitude defined.

VI. Instrument Procedures

Briefings

Each applicant must give a briefing before each takeoff/departure and approach/landing. If the operator, aircraft manufacturer, or training provider has not specified a briefing, the briefing must cover the items appropriate for the conditions, such as: departing/landing runway, departure/arrival procedure, instrument approach procedure, power settings, speeds, missed approach procedures, final approach fix, altitude at final approach fix, initial rate of descent, decision attitude (DA)/decision height (DH)/minimum descent altitude (MDA), time to missed approach, and expectations of the other crewmembers during the approach/landing when in a crew situation. If the applicant provides satisfactory initial takeoff/departure and approach/landing briefings, the evaluator may allow the applicant to brief only the changes, during the remainder of the test. For single-pilot operations, the applicant will verbalize the briefings.

Stabilized Approach Criteria

As used in this ACS, a stabilized approach includes the following components:

- Stable approach speed;
- Stable descent rate;
- Stable vertical flight path; and
- Departure from the final approach fix configured for landing, at the proper approach speed, power setting and flightpath before descending below the minimum stabilized approach height (e.g., 1,000 feet above the airport elevation and at a rate of descent no greater than 1,000 feet per minute unless specifically briefed).

Use of Area Navigation (RNAV) or Required Navigation Performance (RNP) Navigation System

For practical tests conducted in an aircraft equipped with an installed, instrument flight rules (IFR)-approved RNAV or required navigational performance (RNP) system, or in a flight simulation training device (FSTD) equipped to replicate an installed, IFR-approved RNAV or RNP system, the applicant must demonstrate approach proficiency using that system. The applicant may use a suitable RNAV system on conventional procedures and routes as described in the Aeronautical Information Manual (AIM) to accomplish ACS tasks on conventional approach procedures, as appropriate.

Vertical or Lateral Deviation Standard

The standard allows no more than a ¼ scale deflection of either the vertical or lateral deviation indications during the final approach. As markings on flight instruments vary, a ¼ scale deflection of either vertical or lateral guidance is deemed to occur when it is displaced ¼ of the distance that it may be deflected from the indication representing that the aircraft is on the correct flight path.

Task A. Instrument Takeoff

The applicant must encounter Instrument conditions or simulated instrument flight at or before reaching an altitude of 100 feet above airport elevation. In a full flight simulator, the visibility value should be set to no greater than ¼ mile. The applicant must have the ability to control the aircraft, including making the transition to instruments as visual cues deteriorate and can plan and execute the transition to an instrument navigation environment.

Task D. Non-precision Approaches

A non-precision approach is a standard instrument approach procedure to a published minimum descent altitude without approved vertical guidance. The applicant may use navigation systems that display advisory vertical guidance during non-precision approach operations, if available.

The evaluator must select and the applicant must accomplish at least two different non-precision approaches in simulated or actual instrument meteorological conditions:

- At least one procedure must include a course reversal maneuver (e.g., procedure turn, holding in lieu, or the course reversal from an initial approach fix on a Terminal Area Arrival).
- The applicant must accomplish at least one procedure from an initial approach fix without the use of autopilot and without the assistance of radar vectors. During this Task, flying without using the autopilot does not prevent use of the yaw damper and flight director.
- The applicant must fly one procedure with reference to backup or partial panel instrumentation or navigation display, depending on the aircraft's instrument avionics configuration, representing a realistic failure mode(s) for the equipment used.

The evaluator has discretion to have the applicant perform a landing or a missed approach at the completion of each approach.

Task E. Precision Approaches

The applicant must accomplish at least two precision approaches in simulated or actual instrument meteorological conditions to the decision altitude (DA) using aircraft navigational equipment for centerline and vertical guidance.

The applicant must fly at least one procedure without the use of an autopilot and the manually flown segment will begin no later than the Final Approach Fix (FAF). Manually flown precision approaches may use raw data displays or the flight director, at the discretion of the evaluator.

- The applicant should perform one precision approach with reference to backup or partial panel instrumentation or navigation display, depending on the aircraft's instrument avionics configuration, representing realistic failure mode(s) for the equipment used.

- The applicant may fly at least one approach via the autopilot, if equipped, provided the DA/DH does not violate the authorized minimum altitude for autopilot operation.

The evaluator has the discretion to have the applicant perform a landing or missed approach at the completion of each precision approach.

Task F. Landing from a Precision Approach

For evaluations conducted in an airplane, if the applicant has flown the approach to a point where a safe landing and a full stop could have been made but circumstances beyond the control of the applicant prevented an actual landing, the evaluator may give credit for this Task. Credit may also be given for either Task I, Missed Approach or Area of Operation III, Task J, Go-Around/Rejected Landing, provided the applicable Task criteria is met.

Task G. Circling Approach

The approach and landing scenario must include visual maneuvering from the final approach course to a base or downwind leg, as appropriate, for the landing runway. The applicant may circle to land on a runway less than 90-degrees offset from the final approach course provided the applicant makes at least 90-degrees of total heading change(s).

Refer to Appendix 1: Practical Test Roles, Responsibilities, and Outcomes, Circle-to-Land Limitation on an ATP Certificate or Type Rating, for additional information regarding adding or removing this limitation.

Task H. Landing from a Circling Approach

For evaluations conducted in an airplane, if the applicant has flown the approach to a point where a safe landing and a full stop could have been made but circumstances beyond the control of the applicant prevented an actual landing, the evaluator may give credit for this Task. Credit may also be given for either Task I, Missed Approach or Area of Operation III, Task J, Go-Around/Rejected Landing, provided the applicable Task criteria is met.

Refer to Appendix 1: Practical Test Roles, Responsibilities, and Outcomes, Circle-to-Land Limitation on an ATP Certificate or Type Rating, for additional information regarding adding or removing this limitation.

Task I. Missed Approaches

The applicant must perform two missed approaches with at least one being from a precision approach and one consisting of a published missed approach.

One complete published missed approach must be accomplished. Additionally, in multiengine airplanes, a missed approach must be accomplished with one engine inoperative (or simulated inoperative). The engine failure may be experienced any time prior to the initiation of the approach, during the approach, or during the transition to the missed approach attitude and configuration.

Descending below the MDA or continuing a precision approach below DH/DA without the runway environment in sight constitutes unsatisfactory performance. However, even if the applicant initiates a missed approach at the DA/DH, most airplanes briefly descend below DA/DH due to the momentum of the airplane. This descent below DA/DH does not constitute unsatisfactory performance, as long as the descent below the DA/DH does not continue.

VII. Emergency Operations

Task B. Powerplant Failure during Takeoff

In a multiengine airplane certificated with V_1, V_R, or V_2 speeds, a simulated failure of the most critical powerplant should occur at a point:

- after V_1 and prior to V_2, if appropriate under the prevailing conditions in the opinion of the evaluator; or
- as close as possible after V_1 when V_1 and V_2 or V_1 and V_R are identical.

In a multiengine airplane certificated without V_1, V_R, or V_2 speeds, the simulated failure of the most critical powerplant should occur after reaching a minimum of V_{SSE}. If accomplished in the aircraft, the evaluator should not introduce the simulated powerplant failure at an altitude lower than 400 feet AGL. The evaluator should consider local atmospheric conditions, terrain, and aircraft performance available when determining when to simulate the powerplant failure. Tests in an FSTD have no minimum altitude for introducing the powerplant failure.

If a powerplant failure (simulated if in the airplane) occurs after becoming airborne and before reaching an altitude where a safe turn can be made (ASEL, ASES) or the performance capabilities and operating limitations of the airplane will not allow the climb to continue (AMEL, AMES) the applicant should establish a power-off descent approximately straight-ahead.

For a 14 CFR part 25 airplane or an airplane previously certificated as a commuter multiengine airplane under 14 CFR part 23, historical section 23.3(d), if the (simulated) powerplant failure occurs at a point where the airplane can continue to a specified airspeed and altitude at the end of the runway commensurate with the airplane's performance capabilities and operating limitations, the takeoff should be continued (AMEL, AMES).

If available, consult the FSB Report for any considerations in performing this Task in the airplane.

Task C. Powerplant Failure (Simulated) (ASEL, ASES)

No simulated powerplant failure will be given by the evaluator in an airplane when an actual touchdown cannot be safely completed, should it become necessary.

Task D. Powerplant Failure and Restart Procedures (AMEL, AMES)

Refer to Appendix 2: Safety of Flight, Multiengine Airplane Considerations, for additional information concerning required airplane capabilities as they relate to this Task. If the practical test is conducted in a multiengine airplane that requires the pilot to hold a type rating, the applicant may perform a simulated powerplant failure. In this case, a restart procedure must be considered for a given scenario and a simulated restart should be performed, if applicable to the airplane design and the given scenario.

When conducted in an FSTD, feathering or shutdown may be performed in conjunction with any Task and at locations and altitudes at the discretion of the evaluator.

Task E. Approach and Landing with a Powerplant Failure (Simulated) (AMEL, AMES)

For tests conducted in a propeller-driven airplane (other than those that require a type rating), the evaluator will set zero thrust after the applicant has simulated feathering the propeller following a simulated powerplant failure. The applicant must then demonstrate at least one landing with a simulated feathered propeller with the powerplant set to zero thrust. For all other airplanes, follow the manufacturer's recommended procedures.

In airplanes with three powerplants, the applicant must follow a procedure (if approved by the manufacturer and the training program) that approximates the loss of two powerplants, the center and one outboard powerplant. In other multiengine airplanes, the applicant must follow a procedure, which simulates the loss of 50 percent of available powerplants, the loss being simulated on one side of the airplane.

Task F. Precision Approach (Manually Flown) with a Powerplant Failure (Simulated) (AMEL, AMES)

At least one precision approach must be flown without the use of an autopilot. The applicant should begin manually flying prior to the final approach segment. Manually flown precision approaches may use raw data displays or may be flight director assisted, at the discretion of the evaluator. The simulated powerplant failure should occur before initiating the final approach segment and continue to a landing or a missed approach procedure, at the evaluator's discretion.

Task G. Landing from a No Flap or a Nonstandard Flap Approach

This Task is required unless an airplane FSBR has indicated otherwise. The evaluator must determine whether checking on slats only and partial-flap approaches are necessary for the practical test. However, probability of asymmetrical flap failures should be considered in this making this determination.

U.S. Department
of Transportation

**Federal Aviation
Administration**

FAA-G-ACS-2

Airman Certification Standards
Companion Guide for Pilots

November 2023

Flight Standards Service
Washington, DC 20591

Foreword

The Federal Aviation Administration (FAA) developed this Airman Certification Standards Companion Guide FAA-G-ACS-2, for use with the Airman Certification Standards (ACS) for pilot certification. This guide, along with the regulatory material in the ACS, may assist an applicant preparing for the knowledge and practical test(s) that lead to pilot certification. This document is intended only to provide clarity to the public regarding existing requirements under the law or agency policies. The contents of this document do not have the force and effect of law and are not meant to bind the public in any way.

This guide and the ACS are available for download from www.faa.gov.

Comments regarding this document may be emailed to acsptsinquiries@faa.gov.

Revision History

Document #	Description	Date
FAA-G-ACS-2	Airman Certification Standards Companion Guide for Pilots	November 2023

Table of Contents

Why the FAA Created this Guide

The Federal Aviation Administration (FAA) publishes the Airman Certification Standards (ACS) to communicate the aeronautical knowledge, risk management, and flight proficiency standards for various certificates and ratings available to airmen. The ACSs are incorporated by reference into 14 CFR part 61; therefore, the material contained in the ACS is regulatory. This guide, FAA-G-ACS-2, provides additional information to the regulated community to facilitate airman testing. The ACS complies with the safety management system (SMS) framework that the FAA uses to mitigate risks associated with airman certification training and testing. Specifically, the ACS, incorporated by reference (IBR) into the Federal Aviation Regulations, conforms to four functional components of an SMS:

- Safety Policy—Each ACS specifies the Tasks selected by the FAA from the regulatory Areas of Operation. Evaluators formulate a Plan of Action that determines if an applicant can operate safely within the NAS. The ACS represents the FAA's commitment to continually improve safety by including risk management elements in addition to knowledge and skill elements;

- Safety Risk Management that complies with the Administrative Procedures Act (APA) allows the FAA to work with internal and external stakeholders during document formulation. The public at large and stakeholders have an additional chance to provide input during public comment periods;

- Safety Assurance processes ensure a methodical and reasoned incorporation of changes arising from safety recommendations or new developments in aviation; and

- Safety Promotion in the form of engagement and discussion between both external stakeholders (e.g., the aviation training industry) and the FAA policy divisions going forward will determine the content of any ACS that publishes in a Notice of Proposed Rulemaking.

The FAA develops the ACS documents along with associated guidance and updated reference material in collaboration with a diverse group of aviation training experts. The goal is to drive a systematic approach to all components of the airman certification system, including knowledge test question development and conduct of the practical test. The FAA acknowledges and appreciates the many hours that these aviation experts have contributed toward this goal. This level of collaboration, a hallmark of a robust safety culture, strengthens and enhances aviation safety at every level of the airman certification system.

Note: This document does not apply to the Practical Test Standards.

The Non-Regulatory Material in this Guide

This guide provides test preparatory information for an applicant seeking a certificate or rating. This guide also provides a list of references and abbreviations/acronyms used in any ACS and a practical test checklist for use by an applicant. The material in this guide is non-regulatory and may contain terms such as should or may:

- Should indicates actions that are recommended, but not regulatory.

- May is used in a permissive sense to state authority or permission to do the act prescribed.

This document is not legally binding and will not be relied upon by the FAA as a basis for affirmative enforcement action or other administrative penalty. Conformity with the guidance is voluntary only and nonconformity will not affect rights and obligations under existing statutes and regulations.

Section 1: Knowledge Test Eligibility, Description, and Registration

Eligibility

For detailed airman knowledge test eligibility and applicable prerequisites, applicants should refer to the 14 CFR part 61 rules that apply to a specific certificate or rating.

Steps for Knowledge Test Registration

Step 1. Obtain an FAA Tracking Number

The FAA Airman Knowledge Test registration system requires the applicant to have an FAA Tracking Number (FTN). Applicants may obtain an FTN through the Integrated Airman Certification and Rating Application (IACRA) website.

This video describes creating an IACRA account and obtaining an FTN. The specific instructions begin at the 14-minute mark.

Step 2. Create an Account with PSI

After obtaining an FTN, applicants should create an account with the FAA's contracted testing vendor, PSI, a professional testing company which operates hundreds of test centers. Visit PSI's website for information on authorized airman knowledge test centers and how to register, schedule, and pay for an Airman Knowledge Test:

> **Note:** *The IACRA and PSI systems share data that verifies the applicant's FTN and name based on the information input into IACRA by the applicant. The PSI system does not allow applicants to make changes to their name. Applicants who need to make a correction to their name should process that correction in the IACRA system. The applicant's name correction will appear in the PSI system once the applicant logs back into the PSI system and refreshes their account.*

Step 3. Select Test and Testing Center

After obtaining an FTN and creating an account with PSI, applicants may schedule knowledge tests. The PSI system walks the applicant through the process to select a test center in their area and select one or more specific knowledge tests.

Step 4. Select an Available Time Slot

After selecting the test center and test, the applicant may select a date and time slot.

Step 5. Pay for Test

After selecting an available time slot, the PSI system prompts the applicant to pay for the test. After completing this step, the applicant receives an automated email confirmation from PSI.

Applicants are required to meet any applicable Airman Knowledge Test eligibility requirements before arriving at a test center to take a specific knowledge test.

Testing Procedures for Applicants Requesting Special Accommodations

Applicants may request a special accommodation for their airman knowledge test through the PSI test registration and scheduling process. The process allows the applicant to select the specific accommodation(s) needed in accordance with the Americans with Disabilities Act (ADA). The PSI special accommodations team will work with the applicant and the selected testing center to provide appropriate accommodation(s). The PSI special accommodations team may request medical documentation for verification.

Acceptable Forms of Identification

14 CFR part 61, section 61.35, requires an applicant for a knowledge test to have proper identification at the time of application. Before beginning an Airman Knowledge Test, test center personnel will ask to see the applicant's state or federal government-issued photo identification. The identification must contain the applicant's photograph, signature, and date of birth. If the applicant's permanent mailing address is a PO Box number, the applicant must provide a current residential address.

Acceptable Forms of Applicant Address Verification

The table below provides examples of acceptable identification.

All Applicants	U.S. Citizens & Resident Aliens	Non-U.S. Citizens
Identification information must be: ✓ valid ✓ current Identification must include **all** of the following information: ✓ photo ✓ date of birth ✓ signature ✓ physical, residential address	✓ Identification card issued by any **U.S.** state, territory, or government entity (e.g., driver permit or license, government identification card, or military identification card) **or** ✓ Passport **or** ✓ Alien residency card	✓ Passport **and** ✓ Driver permit or license issued by a U.S. state or territory **or** ✓ Identification card issued by any government entity

Airman Knowledge Test Description

The airman knowledge test consists of multiple-choice questions. A single correct response exists for each test question. A correct response to one question does not depend upon, or influence, the correct response to another.

Taking the Knowledge Test

Before starting the actual test, the test center provides an applicant with the opportunity to practice navigating the test software. This practice or tutorial session may include sample questions to familiarize the applicant with the look and feel of the software (e.g., selecting an answer, marking a question for later review, monitoring time remaining for the test, and other features of the testing software). PSI also provides sample tests for registered users on their website.

Acceptable and Unacceptable Materials

The applicant may use the following aids, reference materials, and test materials when taking the knowledge test provided the material does not include actual test questions or answers:

Acceptable Materials	Unacceptable Materials	Notes
Supplement book provided by the proctor	Written materials that are handwritten, printed, or electronic	Testing centers may provide calculators and/or deny the use of personal calculators.
All models of aviation-oriented calculators or small electronic calculators that perform only arithmetic functions	Electronic calculators incorporating permanent or continuous type memory circuits without erasure capability	Proctor may prohibit the use of an applicant's calculator if the proctor is unable to determine the calculator's erasure capability
Calculators with simple programmable memories, which allow the addition to, subtraction from, or retrieval of one number from the memory, or simple functions, such as square root and percentages	Magnetic Cards, magnetic tapes, modules, computer chips, or any other device upon which pre-written programs or information related to the test can be stored and retrieved	Printouts of data should be surrendered at the completion of the test if the calculator incorporates this design feature
Scales, straightedges, protractors, plotters, navigation computers, blank log sheets, holding pattern entry aids, and electronic or mechanical calculators that are directly related to the test	Dictionaries	Before, and upon completion of the test, while in the presence of the proctor, actuate the ON/OFF switch or RESET button, and perform any other function that ensures erasure of any data stored in memory circuits
Manufacturer's permanently inscribed instructions on the front and back of such aids (e.g., formulas, conversions, regulations, signals, weather data, holding pattern diagrams, frequencies, weight and balance formulas, and air traffic control procedures)	Any booklet or manual containing instructions related to the use of test aids	Proctor makes the final determination regarding aids, reference materials, and test materials

Test Taking Tips

When taking a knowledge test, applicants should:

- Read the test instructions carefully;
- Mark difficult questions for later review in order to use the available time efficiently;
- Examine graphs and notes that pertain to the question;
- Request and mark a printed copy of any graph while computing answers, if needed;
- Understand that since only one answer is complete and correct, the other possible answers are either incomplete or erroneous;
- Answer each question in accordance with the current regulations and guidance publications; and
- Answer all the questions before time allotted for the test expires.
- Review 14 CFR part 61, section 61.37 regarding cheating or other unauthorized conduct.

Section 2: Airman Knowledge Test Report

Upon completion of the knowledge test, the test center issues a printed Airman Knowledge Test Report (AKTR) to the applicant, which documents the applicant's test score and lists a code for any questions answered incorrectly. The applicant should retain the original AKTR. During the oral portion of a practical test, the evaluator reviews the AKTR, and assesses any noted areas of deficiency.

Applicant Name Considerations for the Airman Knowledge Test Report and the Practical Test

The FAA compares the applicant's name on the AKTR with the name on the practical test application form when examining certificate and rating applications and before issuing a permanent certificate to the applicant. If an incorrect middle initial, spelling variant, or different middle name is on the AKTR or if there is a first name variation of any kind between the AKTR and the formal application for a certificate or rating, the evaluator for the practical test should attach an explanation and a copy of the applicant's photo identification to the IACRA or paper application. An IACRA application cannot be processed if the applicant's last name or suffix (e.g., Jr., Sr.) on the AKTR does not match the name recorded on the application form. In this case, the applicant should use a paper application, and the evaluator should include an explanation and copy of the applicant's photo identification to avoid a correction notice.

Retesting After Failure of AKTR

An applicant retesting after the failure of any Airman Knowledge Test may retest with appropriate authorization. The applicant should bring the applicable AKTR indicating failure to the test center, along with an endorsement from an Authorized Instructor who gave the applicant the required additional training in accordance with 14 CFR part 61, section 61.49. The endorsement certifies that the applicant is competent to pass the knowledge test.

Knowledge Test Codes During Transition from PTS To ACS

When a PTS is the effective standard for a specific certificate or rating, the applicant receives an Airman Knowledge Test Report with pilot (PLT) codes that correspond to any knowledge test question(s) the applicant answered incorrectly. For example: PLT044.

For knowledge tests taken after an ACS becomes the effective standard for a specific certificate or rating, the test center issues an AKTR with ACS codes that correspond to any knowledge test question(s) the applicant answered incorrectly. For example: CA.I.A.K1

During a period of transition after an ACS replaces a PTS, an applicant could possess a valid AKTR with PLT codes. When this occurs, instructors and evaluators can continue to use PLT codes in conjunction with the appropriate ACS for targeting training and retesting of missed knowledge subject areas by looking up the PLT code(s) in the Learning Statement Reference Guide.

After noting the subject area(s) for the PLT codes, instructors and evaluators should check or test the applicant's understanding of that material in the context of the appropriate ACS Area(s) of Operation and Task(s).

> **Note:** Test codes for the Fundamentals of Instructing knowledge test are the same for all instructor certificates and will issue with ACS codes after the first instructor ACS becomes effective.

ACS Archived Test Codes

As a result of updates made to an ACS, an AKTR may contain one or more archived ACS codes. These codes are indicated as archived within the ACS. For example:

PA.VIII.E.K1a   Archived.

Use of archived codes in the ACS avoids code shifting that could create ambiguity when looking up ACS codes listed on an AKTR. An unexpired AKTR may span ACS revisions and ACS codes may archive after an applicant takes a knowledge test. Therefore, an applicant, instructor, or evaluator may need to interpret one or more archived ACS codes on an AKTR. Individuals can refer to the ACS revision in effect on the date of the knowledge test or to section 8 of this guide for archived ACS codes and the associated element text.

Use of archived codes in the ACS avoids code shifting that could create ambiguity when looking up ACS codes listed on an AKTR. An unexpired AKTR may span ACS revisions and ACS codes may archive after an applicant takes a knowledge test. Therefore, an applicant, instructor, or evaluator may need to interpret one or more archived ACS codes on an AKTR. Individuals can refer to the ACS revision in effect on the date of the knowledge test or to Section 8 of this guide for archived ACS codes and the associated element text. For example, the archived ACS code for Private Pilot Airplane element PA.VIII.E.K1a is noted in Section 8 of this guide as: Sensitivity, limitations, and potential errors in unusual attitudes.

Obtaining a Duplicate AKTR

If the applicant's knowledge test was taken on or after January 13, 2020, the applicant can print a duplicate or expired test report (AKTR) by visiting the PSI website.

If the knowledge test was taken on or before January 10, 2020, the applicant should follow 14 CFR, section 61.29 for replacement of a lost or destroyed AKTR.

Section 3: ACS Risk Management

Risk management involves perception of hazards, the ability to process the probability and severity of outcomes associated with any hazard, and performance of appropriate risk mitigation as needed to preserve the desired margin of safety.

Previous editions of the ACS often used elements for evaluation of risk management as encompassing a failure to do something. Many of these "failure to act" elements mimicked skill elements and limited an evaluator's opportunity to thoroughly examine an applicant's understanding of risk management.

For example, see elements R1 and S2 from the Private Pilot — Airplane Airman Certification Standards (FAA-S-ACS-6B with Change 1) in the excerpt below:

Task	C. Systems and Equipment Malfunctions
References	FAA-H-8083-2, FAA-H-8083-3; POH/AFM
Objective	To determine that the applicant exhibits satisfactory knowledge, risk management, and skills associated with system and equipment malfunctions appropriate to the airplane provided for the practical test and analyzing the situation and take appropriate action for simulated emergencies.
Knowledge	The applicant demonstrates understanding of:
PA.IX.C.K1	Partial or complete power loss related to the specific powerplant, including:
PA.IX.C.K1a	a. Engine roughness or overheat
PA.IX.C.K1b	b. Carburetor or induction icing
PA.IX.C.K1c	c. Loss of oil pressure
PA.IX.C.K1d	d. Fuel starvation
PA.IX.C.K2	System and equipment malfunctions specific to the airplane, including:
PA.IX.C.K2a	a. Electrical malfunction
PA.IX.C.K2b	b. Vacuum/pressure and associated flight instrument malfunctions
PA.IX.C.K2c	c. Pitot/static system malfunction
PA.IX.C.K2d	d. Electronic flight deck display malfunction
PA.IX.C.K2e	e. Landing gear or flap malfunction
PA.IX.C.K2f	f. Inoperative trim
PA.IX.C.K3	Smoke/fire/engine compartment fire.
PA.IX.C.K4	Any other system specific to the airplane (e.g., supplemental oxygen, deicing).
PA.IX.C.K5	Inadvertent door or window opening.
Risk Management	The applicant demonstrates the ability to identify, assess and mitigate risks, encompassing:
PA.IX.C.R1	Failure to use the proper checklist for a system or equipment malfunction.
PA.IX.C.R2	Distractions, loss of situational awareness, or improper task management.
Skills	The applicant demonstrates the ability to:
PA.IX.C.S1	Describe appropriate action for simulated emergencies specified by the evaluator, from at least three of the elements or sub-elements listed in K1 through K5 above.
PA.IX.C.S2	Complete the appropriate checklist.

The FAA reworded risk elements that describe a Failure to... (or similar phrases) with language permitting an open-ended examination of risk management by the evaluator. See element R2 in the excerpt below (image for illustration purposes only):

Task C. Systems and Equipment Malfunctions	
References: FAA-H-8083-2, FAA-H-8083-3, FAA-H-8083-25; POH/AFM	
Objective: To determine the applicant exhibits satisfactory knowledge, risk management, and skills associated with system and equipment malfunctions appropriate to the airplane provided for the practical test.	
Knowledge:	The applicant demonstrates understanding of:
PA.IX.C.K1	Causes of partial or complete power loss related to the specific type of powerplant(s).
PA.IX.C.K1a	a. [Archived]
PA.IX.C.K1b	b. [Archived]
PA.IX.C.K1c	c. [Archived]
PA.IX.C.K1d	d. [Archived]
PA.IX.C.K2	System and equipment malfunctions specific to the aircraft, including:
PA.IX.C.K2a	a. Electrical malfunction
PA.IX.C.K2b	b. Vacuum/pressure and associated flight instrument malfunctions
PA.IX.C.K2c	c. Pitot-static system malfunction
PA.IX.C.K2d	d. Electronic flight deck display malfunction
PA.IX.C.K2e	e. Landing gear or flap malfunction
PA.IX.C.K2f	f. Inoperative trim
PA.IX.C.K3	Causes and remedies for smoke or fire onboard the aircraft.
PA.IX.C.K4	Any other system specific to the aircraft (e.g., supplemental oxygen, deicing).
PA.IX.C.K5	Inadvertent door or window opening.
Risk Management:	The applicant is able to identify, assess, and mitigate risk associated with:
PA.IX.C.R1	Checklist usage for a system or equipment malfunction.
PA.IX.C.R2	Distractions, task prioritization, loss of situational awareness, or disorientation.
PA.IX.C.R3	Undesired aircraft state.
PA.IX.C.R4	Startle response.
Skills:	The applicant exhibits the skill to:
PA.IX.C.S1	Determine appropriate action for simulated emergencies specified by the evaluator, from at least three of the elements or sub-elements listed in K1 through K5.
PA.IX.C.S2	Complete the appropriate checklist(s).

Section 4: Flight Instructor Applicant Considerations

Flight Instructor ACS Information

Flight Instructor ACS documents include sections that define the acceptable standards for knowledge, risk management, and skills unique to an instructor certificate or rating.

Knowledge elements often begin with "The applicant demonstrates instructional knowledge by describing and explaining..." Instructional knowledge means the instructor applicant can effectively present the what, how, and why involved with the task elements using techniques described in the fundamentals of instructing (FOI) area of operation in an instructor ACS.

The Fundamentals of Instructing (FOI), Area of Operation I, Task F: Elements of Effective Teaching that include Risk Management and Accident Prevention focuses on teaching risk management and on those risks encountered by a flight instructor while providing in-flight instruction.

Instructor applicants deal with additional risk management on several levels. These include teaching risk management in the classroom and mitigation of risk during flight instruction.

Note that the FOI sections in each instructor ACS are identical and use the same element codes. This makes it possible to use the same FOI elements for every instructor ACS.

Section 5: References

The ACS are based on the following 14 CFR parts, FAA guidance documents, manufacturer's publications, and other documents.

Note: *Users should reference the current edition of the reference documents listed below. The current edition of all FAA publications can be found at <u>www.faa.gov</u>.*

Reference	Title
14 CFR part 1	Definitions and Abbreviations
14 CFR part 23	Airworthiness Standards: Normal Category Airplanes
14 CFR part 25	Airworthiness Standards: Transport Category Airplanes
14 CFR part 27	Airworthiness Standards: Normal Category Rotorcraft
14 CFR part 29	Airworthiness Standards: Transport Category Rotorcraft
14 CFR part 39	Airworthiness Directives
14 CFR part 43	Maintenance, Preventive Maintenance, Rebuilding, and Alteration
14 CFR part 61	Certification: Pilots, Flight Instructors, and Ground Instructors
14 CFR part 63	Certification: Flight Crewmembers other than Pilots
14 CFR part 65	Certification: Airmen Other Than Flightcrew Members
14 CFR part 67	Medical Standards and Certification
14 CFR part 68	Requirements for Operating Certain Small Aircraft Without a Medical Certificate
14 CFR part 71	Designation of Class A, B, C, D, and E Airspace Areas; Air Traffic Service Routes; and Reporting Points
14 CFR part 91	General Operating and Flight Rules
14 CFR part 93	Special Air Traffic Rules
14 CFR part 97	Standard Instrument Procedures
14 CFR part 117	Flight and Duty Limitations and Rest Requirements: Flightcrew Members
14 CFR part 119	Certification: Air Carriers and Commercial Operators
14 CFR part 121	Operating Requirements: Domestic, Flag, and Supplemental Operations
14 CFR part 135	Operating Requirements: Commuter and on Demand Operations and Rules Governing Persons on Board Such Aircraft
49 CFR part 830	Notification and Reporting of Aircraft Accidents or Incidents and Overdue Aircraft, and Preservation of Aircraft Wreckage, Mail, Cargo, and Records
AC 00-30	Clear Air Turbulence Avoidance
AC 00-46	Aviation Safety Reporting Program
AC 20-117	Hazards Following Ground Deicing and Ground Operations in Conditions Conducive to Aircraft Icing
AC 29-2	Certification of Transport Category Rotorcraft
AC 60-22	Aeronautical Decision Making
AC 60-28	FAA English Language Standard for an FAA Certificate Issued Under 14 CFR Parts 61, 63, 65, and 107
AC 61-65	Certification: Pilots and Flight and Ground Instructors

Reference	Title
AC 61-67	Stall and Spin Awareness Training
AC 61-107	Aircraft Operations at Altitudes Above 25,000 Feet Mean Sea Level or Mach Numbers Greater Than .75
AC 61-138	Airline Transport Pilot Certification Training Program
AC 61-140	Autorotation Training
AC 68-1	BasicMed
AC 90-48	Pilots' Role in Collision Avoidance
AC 90-95	Unanticipated Right Yaw in Helicopters
AC 90-100	U.S Terminal and En Route Area Navigation (RNAV) Operations
AC 90-105	Approval Guidance for RNP Operations and Barometric Vertical Navigation in the U.S. National Airspace System and in Oceanic and Remote Continental Airspace
AC 90-107	Guidance for Localizer Performance with Vertical Guidance and Localizer Performance without Vertical Guidance Approach Operations in the U.S. National Airspace System
AC 90-117	Data Link Communications
AC 91.21-1	Use of Portable Electronic Devices Aboard Aircraft
AC 91-32	Safety in and Around Helicopters
AC 91-55	Reduction of Electrical System Failures Following Aircraft Engine Starting
AC 91-73	Parts 91 and 135 Single Pilot, Flight School Procedures During Taxi Operations
AC 91-74	Pilot Guide: Flight in Icing Conditions
AC 91-78	Use of Class 1 or Class 2 Electronic Flight Bag (EFB)
AC 91-79	Mitigating the Risks of a Runway Overrun Upon Landing
AC 91-92	Pilot's Guide to a Preflight Briefing
AC 120-27	Aircraft Weight and Balance Control
AC 120-51	Crew Resource Management Training
AC 120-57	Surface Movement Guidance and Control System
AC 120-58	Pilot Guide Large Aircraft Ground Deicing
AC 120-60	Ground Deicing and Anti-icing Program
AC 120-66	Aviation Safety Action Program (ASAP)
AC 120-71	Standard Operating Procedures and Pilot Monitoring Duties for Flight Deck Crewmembers
AC 120-74	Parts 91, 121, 125, and 135 Flightcrew Procedures During Taxi Operations
AC 120-76	Authorization for Use of Electronic Flight Bags
AC 120-82	Flight Operational Quality Assurance (FOQA)
AC 120-90	Line Operations Safety Audit (LOSA)
AC 120-100	Basics of Aviation Fatigue
AC 120-101	Part 121 Air Carrier Operational Control
AC 120-108	Continuous Descent Final Approach

Reference	Title
AC 120-109	Stall Prevention and Recovery Training
AC 120-111	Upset Prevention and Recovery Training
AC 135-17	Pilot Guide - Small Aircraft Ground Deicing
AFM	Airplane Flight Manual
AIM	Aeronautical Information Manual
AC 120-100	Basics of Aviation Fatigue
AC 120-101	Part 121 Air Carrier Operational Control
AC 120-108	Continuous Descent Final Approach
AC 120-109	Stall Prevention and Recovery Training
AC 120-111	Upset Prevention and Recovery Training
AC 135-17	Pilot Guide - Small Aircraft Ground Deicing
AFM	Airplane Flight Manual
AIM	Aeronautical Information Manual
Applicable Manufacturer's Equipment Supplement(s)	Manufacturer's Equipment Supplement(s)
Appropriate Manufacturer's Safety Notices	Safety Notices
Chart Supplements	Chart Supplements
Digital-Visual Charts (d-VC)	Digital-Visual Charts (d-VC)
FAA-H-8083-1	Aircraft Weight and Balance Handbook
FAA-H-8083-2	Risk Management Handbook
FAA-H-8083-3	Airplane Flying Handbook
FAA-H-8083-9	Aviation Instructor's Handbook
FAA-H-8083-15	Instrument Flying Handbook
FAA-H-8083-16	Instrument Procedures Handbook
FAA-H-8083-21	Helicopter Flying Handbook
FAA-H-8083-23	Seaplane, Skiplane, and Float/Ski Equipped Helicopter Operations Handbook
FAA-H-8083-25	Pilot's Handbook of Aeronautical Knowledge
FAA-H-8083-28	Aviation Weather Handbook
FAA Order 8130.2	Airworthiness Certification of Aircraft
FAA-P-8740-66	Flying Light Twins Safely
FSB Report (type specific)	Flight Standardization Board Report (if available)
Helicopter Route Charts	Helicopter Route Charts
IFR Enroute Charts	IFR Enroute Low Altitude and IFR Enroute High Altitude Charts
NOTAMs	Notices to Air Missions
PDC	Profile Descent Charts

Reference	Title
POH/AFM	Pilot's Operating Handbook/FAA-Approved Airplane Flight Manual
POH/Flight Manual	Pilot's Operating Handbook/FAA-Approved Flight Manual
POH/RFM	Pilot's Operating Handbook/FAA-Approved Rotorcraft Flight Manual
QRH	Quick Reference Handbook
SAFO 16016	Helicopter Stabilized Hover Checks Before Departure
SAFO 17010	Incorrect Airport Surface Approaches and Landings
SAFO 19001	Landing Performance Assessments at Time of Arrival
STARs	Standard Terminal Arrival Routes
TPP	Terminal Procedures Publications
USCG Navigation Rules	USCG Navigation Rules, International-Inland
VFR Navigation Charts	Sectional/Terminal Aeronautical Charts

Section 6: Abbreviations and Acronyms

Note: *Users should reference the current edition of the reference documents listed below. The current edition of all FAA publications can be found at www.faa.gov.*

Acronym	Description
14 CFR	Title 14 of the Code of Federal Regulations
AATD	Advanced Aviation Training Device
AC	Advisory Circular
ACS	Airman Certification Standards
ADM	Aeronautical Decision-Making
ADS-B	Automatic Dependent Surveillance Broadcast
ADS-C	Automatic Dependent Surveillance - Contract
AFCS	Automatic Flight Control System
AFM	Airplane Flight Manual
AGL	Above Ground Level
AIM	Aeronautical Information Manual
AIRMET	Airman's Meteorological Information
AKTR	Airman Knowledge Test Report
AMEL	Airplane Multiengine Land
AMES	Airplane Multiengine Sea
APU	Auxiliary Power Unit
ASEL	Airplane Single-Engine Land
ASES	Airplane Single-Engine Sea
ASI	Aviation Safety Inspector
ATC	Air Traffic Control
ATD	Aviation Training Device
ATP	Airline Transport Pilot
BATD	Basic Aviation Training Device
CDI	Course Deviation Indicator
CDL	Configuration Deviation List
CFIT	Controlled Flight Into Terrain
CFR	Code of Federal Regulations
CG	Center of Gravity
CPDLC	Controller–pilot data link communication
CRM	Crew Resource Management
DA	Decision Altitude
DDA	Derived Decision Altitude

Acronym	Description
DH	Decision Height
DME	Distance Measuring Equipment
DP	Departure Procedures
EFB	Electronic Flight Bag
EFC	Expect Further Clearance
EFIS	Electronic Flight Instrument System
ELT	Emergency Locator Transmitter
ETA	Estimated Time of Arrival
ETL	Effective Translational Lift
FAA	Federal Aviation Administration
FAF	Final Approach Fix
FB	Wind and Temperature Aloft Forecast
FFS	Full Flight Simulator
FMS	Flight Management System
FRAT	Flight Risk Assessment Tool
FSB	Flight Standardization Board
FSO	Flight Standards Office
FSTD	Flight Simulation Training Device
FTD	Flight Training Device
G	Unit of Force Equal to Earth's Gravity
GBAS	Ground Based Augmentation System
GFA	Graphical Forecast for Aviation
GNSS	Global Navigation Satellite System
GPS	Global Positioning System
H/V	Height/Velocity
HF	High Frequency
HIGE	Hover in Ground Effect
HUD	Head Up Display
IFR	Instrument Flight Rules
ILS	Instrument Landing System
IMC	Instrument Meteorological Conditions
INFO	Information for Operators
INS	Inertial Navigation System
IOS	Instructor Operating Station
KOEL	Kinds of Operations Equipment List
L/DMAX	Lift/Drag Maximum

Acronym	Description
LAHSO	Land and Hold Short Operations
LNAV	Lateral Navigation
LOA	Letter of Authorization
LOC-I	Loss of Control in Flight
LP	Localizer Performance
LTE	Loss of Tail Rotor Effectiveness
LTM	Long Term Memory
MAP	Missed Approach Point
MDA	Minimum Descent Altitude
MEL	Minimum Equipment List
METAR	Aviation Routine Weather Reports (Meteorological Aerodrome Report)
MFD	Multi-Function Display
MMO	Maximum Operating Limit Speed as a Mach Number
NAS	National Airspace System
NOTAM	Notice to Air Missions
Nr	Main Rotor Speed
NSP	National Simulator Program
NTSB	National Transportation Safety Board
ODP	Obstacle Departure Procedure
OEI	One Engine Inoperative
PAVE	Risk Management Checklist for Pilot/Aircraft/enVironment/External Factors
PFD	Primary Flight Display
PIC	Pilot-in-Command
PinS	Copter Point in Space
PIREP	Pilot Report
POA	Plan of Action
POH	Pilot's Operating Handbook
PTS	Practical Test Standards
QPS	Qualification Performance Standard
QRH	Quick Reference Handbook
RAIM	Receiver Autonomous Integrity Monitoring
RCAM	Runway Condition Assessment Matrix
RFM	Rotorcraft Flight Manual
RNAV	Area Navigation
RNP	Required Navigation Performance
RPM	Revolutions Per Minute

Acronym	Description
SAE	Specialty Aircraft Examiner
SAFO	Safety Alert for Operators
SATR	Special Air Traffic Rules
SBAS	Satellite Based Augmentation System
SBT	Scenario Based Training
SFAR	Special Federal Aviation Regulation
SFRA	Special Flight Rules Area
SID	Standard Instrument Departure
SIGMET	Significant Meteorological Information
SMS	Safety Management System
SRM	Single-Pilot Resource Management
SRM	Safety Risk Management
STAR	Standard Terminal Arrival
STM	Short Term Memory
SUA	Special Use Airspace
TAF	Terminal Area Forecast
TAWS	Terrain Awareness and Warning System
TCAS	Traffic Collision Avoidance System
TCDS	Type Certificate Data Sheet
TCE	Training Center Evaluator
TEM	Threat and Error Management
TFR	Temporary Flight Restrictions
TPP	Terminal Procedures Publication
TUC	Time of Useful Consciousness
UHF	Ultra High Frequency
UIMC	Unintended Instrument Meteorological Conditions
USCG	United States Coast Guard
UTC	Coordinated Universal Time
V_1	The maximum speed in the takeoff at which the pilot must take the first action (e.g., apply brakes, reduce thrust, deploy speed brakes) to stop the airplane within the accelerate-stop distance. V_1 also means the minimum speed in the takeoff, following a failure of the critical engine at V_{EF}, at which the pilot can continue the takeoff and achieve the required height above the takeoff surface within the takeoff distance.
V_2	Takeoff Safety Speed
V_A	Maneuvering speed
VDP	Visual Descent Point
VFR	Visual Flight Rules

Acronym	Description
V_{MC}	Minimum control speed with the critical engine inoperative
VHF	Very High Frequency
VMC	Visual Meteorological Conditions
V_{MCG}	Minimum control speed on the ground with the critical engine inoperative
V_{MO}	Maximum Operating Limit Speed
V_{NE}	Never exceed speed
VCOA	Visual Climb Over Airport
VOR	Very High Frequency Omnidirectional Range
V_R	Rotation speed
V_{REF}	Reference Landing Speed
VRS	Vortex Ring State
V_S	Stall Speed
V_{SO}	Stalling Speed or the Minimum Steady Flight Speed in the Landing Configuration
V_{SSE}	Safe, intentional one-engine-inoperative speed. Originally known as safe single-engine speed
VTOL	Vertical Takeoff and Landing
V_X	Best angle of climb airspeed
V_{XSE}	Best angle of climb speed with one engine inoperative
V_Y	Best rate of climb speed
V_{YSE}	Best rate of climb speed with one engine inoperative.
WAAS	Wide Area Augmentation System

Section 7: Practical Test Checklist (Applicant)

Evaluator's Name: _____

Location: _____

Date/Time: _____

Acceptable Aircraft

- ☐ Aircraft Documents:

  - ☐ Airworthiness Certificate

  - ☐ Registration Certificate

  - ☐ Operating Limitations

- ☐ Aircraft Maintenance Records:

  - ☐ Logbook Record of Airworthiness Inspections and Airworthiness Directives (AD) Compliance

- ☐ Pilot's Operating Handbook and FAA-Approved Aircraft Flight Manual

Personal Equipment

- ☐ View-Limiting Device

- ☐ Current Aeronautical Charts (printed or electronic)

- ☐ Computer and Plotter

- ☐ Flight Plan Form and Flight Logs (printed or electronic)

- ☐ Chart Supplements, Airport Diagrams, and Appropriate Publications (printed or electronic)

- ☐ Current AIM (printed or electronic)

Personal Records

- ☐ Government-Issued Identification—Photo/Signature Identification (ID)

- ☐ Pilot Certificate

- ☐ Current Medical Certificate or BasicMed Qualification (when applicable)

- ☐ Completed FAA Form 8710-1, Airman Certificate and/or Rating Application, or completed IACRA form, FAA Form 8710-11, Airman Certificate and/or Rating Application—Sport Pilot, or FAA Form 8400.3, Airman Certificate and/or Rating Application with Instructor's Signature, if applicable

- ☐ Airman Knowledge Test Report

- ☐ Airman's Logbook with Appropriate Instructor Endorsements

- ☐ FAA Form 8060-5, Notice of Disapproval (if applicable)

- ☐ Letter of Discontinuance (if applicable)

- ☐ Approved School Graduation Certificate (if applicable)

Section 8: Knowledge Test Reports and Archived ACS Codes

Private Pilot for Airplane Category ACS Archived Codes

PA.III.A.R3	Confirmation or expectation bias.
PA.IV.A.S10	Retract the water rudders, as appropriate, establish and maintain the most efficient planing/liftoff attitude, and correct for porpoising and skipping (ASES, AMES).
PA.IV.I.S5	Retract the water rudders as appropriate; advance the throttle smoothly to takeoff power.
PA.IV.K.S7	Retract the water rudders as appropriate; advance the throttle smoothly to takeoff power.
PA.VIII.E.K1a	Sensitivity, limitations, and potential errors in unusual attitudes
PA.VIII.E.K1b	Correlation (pitch instruments/bank instruments)
PA.VIII.E.K1c	Function and operation
PA.VIII.E.K1d	Proper instrument cross-check techniques
PA.VIII.E.R2	Failure to seek assistance or declare an emergency in a deteriorating situation.
PA.VIII.E.R6	Failure to unload the wings in recovering from high G situations.
PA.VIII.F.S3	Maintain altitude ±200 feet, heading ±20°, and airspeed ±10 knots.
PA.IX.C.K1a	Maintain altitude ±200 feet, heading ±20°, and airspeed ±10 knots
PA.IX.C.K1b	Engine roughness or overheat
PA.IX.C.K1c	Loss of oil pressure
PA.IX.C.K1d	Fuel starvation
PA.XII.A.R2	Confirmation or expectation bias as related to taxi instructions.
PA.XII.A.S1	Demonstrate runway incursion avoidance procedures.
PA.XII.B.R2	Confirmation or expectation bias as related to taxi instructions.

Commercial Pilot for Airplane Category ACS Archived Codes

CA.I.F.K2f   Weight and balance

CA.IV.A.S10   Retract the water rudders, as appropriate, establish and maintain the most efficient planing/liftoff attitude, and correct for porpoising and skipping (ASES, AMES).

CA.IV.I.S5   Retract the water rudders as appropriate; advance the throttle smoothly to takeoff power.

CA.IV.K.S7   Retract the water rudders as appropriate; advance the throttle smoothly to takeoff power.

CA.IV.B.S5   Recognize signal loss or interference and take appropriate action, if applicable.

CA.IX.C.K1a   Engine roughness or overheat

CA.IX.C.K1b   Carburetor or induction icing

CA.IX.C.K1c   Loss of oil pressure

CA.IX.C.K1d   Fuel starvation

CA.XI.A.R2   Confirmation or expectation bias as related to taxi instructions.

CA.XI.A.S1   Utilize runway incursion avoidance procedures.

CA.XI.B.R2   Confirmation or expectation bias as related to taxi instructions.

Instrument Rating – Airplane ACS Archived Codes

IR.IV.B.R2   Failure to recognize an unusual flight attitude and follow the proper recovery procedure.

IR.VII.C.R2   Collision hazards, to include aircraft, terrain, obstacles, wires, vehicles, vessels, persons, and wildlife.

Airline Transport Pilot and Type Rating ACS Archived Codes

AA.IV.B.R2   Failure to recognize an unusual flight attitude and follow the proper recovery procedure.

AA.V.A.S2   When accomplished in an FSTD, the entry should be consistent with the expected operational environment for a stall on takeoff or while on approach in a partial flap configuration with no minimum entry altitude defined.

AA.V.B.S2   When accomplished in an FSTD, the entry should be consistent with the expected operational environment for a stall in cruise flight with no minimum entry altitude defined.

AA.V.C.S2   When accomplished in an FSTD, the entry should be consistent with the expected operational environment for a stall when fully configured for landing with no minimum entry altitude defined.

AA.VI.F.R3   Planning for.

AA.VI.F.R3a   a. Missed Approach

AA.VI.F.R3b   b. Land and hold short operations (LAHSO)

AA.VI.H.R3   Planning for.

AA.VI.H.R3a   a. Missed Approach

AA.VI.H.R3b   b. Land and hold short operations (LAHSO)

AA.VIII.A.R2   Confirmation or expectation bias as related to taxi instructions.

AA.VIII.B.R2   Confirmation or expectation bias as related to taxi instructions.